Wisconsin Dells

Wisconsin Dells

A Guide for Tourists

Dirk Vander Wilt

Wisconsin Dells: a Guide for Tourists
Text © 2006 by Dirk Vander Wilt
Photos and maps © 2006 by Dirk Vander Wilt
(unless otherwise noted)

Published by Parkscape Press
an imprint of Channel Lake, Inc.

New York, NY
Published in February, 2006
Version 1.0.0

ISBN: 0-9767064-2-3
Library of Congress Control Number: 2005910153

For more information, visit: http://www.parkscapepress.com

For Emily

Table of Contents

TABLE OF CONTENTS   **7**

INTRODUCTION   **11**
The Purpose of this Book   12

THE AMERICAN VACATION   **16**

WHY VISIT WISCONSIN DELLS?   **33**
the Dells of the Wisconsin River   33
History of the Dells   34
Detour: Mytholical Inhabitants   38
Famous Residents   40
Who Visits Wisconsin Dells   42
Orientation   43
Things to do in Wisconsin Dells   45
Natural Features   47
Getting There   48
Getting Around   49
Spending the Night   50
Dells Seasons   51

DELLS EARLY PHOTOGRAPHY   **54**
Stereoscopic Photography   54
Panoramic Photography   55
H. H. Bennett   56

DELLS TOURS   **64**
Duck & Boat Tours   64
Other Dells Experiences   69

THE PARKS & RESORTS   **70**
Water & Amusement Parks   72
Waterpark Resorts   77
Major Indoor Waterpark Resorts   78
Hotels with Water Activities   82

ANIMALS AND NATURE   85
Horseback Riding   85
Animal Encounters   87
Boating and Fishing   88
State Parks   91

AREA ATTRACTIONS   93
Museums   93
Walk-Through Attractions   95
Train Experiences   100
Live Shows   101
Fun for Grown-Ups   104
Golf Courses   107
Fudge and Sweets   108
Other Fun Things   110
Detour: Politics of Peck   111

EATING AND SLEEPING   117
Restaurants   117
Area Restaurants   117
Downtown Restaurants & Bars   118
Accommodations   119
Wisconsin Dells Parkway   119
Commercial Campgrounds   121
Downtown Dells Area   123

NEARBY ATTRACTIONS   125
Other Area Attractions   125
Madison   127

THE HOUSE ON THE ROCK   129
What is the House?   129
History   130
Touring the House   132
Resort Complex   134
Conclusion   136

TRAVEL SCENARIOS 137

AUTHOR RECOMMENDATIONS 140

RESEARCH 143
Books 143
Websites 144
List of Attractions 145
List of Historic Photographs 148
Index 150

Wisconsin Dells Area Map
Lake Delton - Wisconsin Dells Parkway - Downtown Dells
Upper & Lower Dells - Interstate 90/94

North

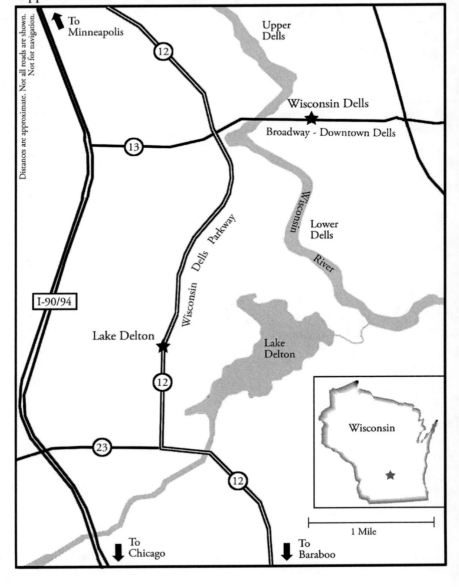

Introduction

I have written my share of travel guides about tourist traps and fun vacation destinations. I have explored these towns across America, trying to pick and choose between which ones deserve a travel guide.

But this one is special. I have been intentionally avoiding writing this book because Wisconsin Dells means much more to me than just another town-of-billboards. It is my home turf. Being born and raised in Chicagoland, I have been to Wisconsin Dells dozens of times, from as young as I can remember. I went on my first waterslide here. I rode my first roller coaster and explored my first wax museum here. This town is why I love kitsch so much.

When I relocated to New York City as an adult to pursue my various academic and professional endeavors, I spent years looking for a nearby town comparable to the Dells. But I never found it. Lake George, Atlantic City, and Niagara Falls are all great vacation destinations, but they just don't have the same classic American luster as the Dells.

My first memory of Wisconsin Dells is playing at Noah's Ark (the waterpark), and riding my first waterslide. Before then, I was too scared. I was about ten years old, and I must have ridden twenty times around a lazy river on that day. My brother – three years younger than me, I might add – went down a nearby waterslide many times. I remember thinking that the slide must have been ten stories high (though I'm sure it wasn't). I finally mustered up the courage to join him on the long climb up the staircase to the loading bay. Then, for some reason, I went down the slide right after him… and I loved it! I went on that waterslide many more times; and on as many other slides as I could manage to fit into the day. If you ever come with me to the Dells, I'll show you the exact lazy river and exact waterslide that changed my life forever.

I also had my first Ripley's experience at the Dells. When I was young, I didn't care much about the individual exhibits; I don't think I read a single information plaque during my entire first venture. What I loved was the environments that Ripley's created; one moment I was in a cave, and the next I was in a spooky cemetery. Of course in my more mature treks I actually read and learned about the exhibits (which probably shows the wide range people that can enjoy a Ripley's museum). Perhaps it is no coincidence that nearly every tourist town I decide to write about contains a Ripley's *Believe it or Not!* Museum. For me, it all came from Wisconsin Dells.

Alright, now that I've successfully built up the Dells so much that it cannot possibly live up to this expectation… just be prepared for a skyline of roller coasters, waterparks, gift shops, and motels. I hope you enjoy touring this town as much as I do!

THE PURPOSE OF THIS BOOK

This section answers a few of the common questions about the choices the author made with regard to the attractions, recommendations, and more.

How do you decide which attractions are included?
This book is not all-inclusive. I repeat: this book is *not* all-inclusive. It is comprehensive, with many different options for entertainment, dining, eating, shopping, etc., but there are many establishments in Wisconsin Dells not listed here. Since this is an independent guide, and no payment of any kind was accepted for inclusion herein, the decision of what to include was made entirely by the author.

How is this book organized?
This book has a structure designed to allow for coherent perusal. However, because of the sheer diversity of the attractions within Wisconsin Dells, some editorial decisions had to be made on what to include and where.

Nonetheless, here is the formula: the attractions are listed by type, such as whether they revolve around the Dells themselves, or on other cultural or historical diversions. If you absolutely cannot find an entry in any section that you are sure is in the book, refer to the appendices, or the "Index of Attractions" at the end of this book, which lists the page numbers and attraction names of everything contained herein.

What is an "attraction"?

This book makes references to "attractions." So what does that mean? Are they restaurants? Amusement parks? Hotels? Casinos? Attractions are all those things! Anything that might bring a visitor to Wisconsin Dells is an attraction.

How much does an attraction cost?

At the end of each attraction listing is a general pricing reference, indicated by dollar signs. This is meant as a general reference, based on the general adult admission price:

"$"	=	Less than $10
"$$"	=	$10-$25
"$$$"	=	$25-$50
"$$$$"	=	over $50
No "$"	=	No price info

What about "Seasonal" attractions?

Wisconsin Dells used to be all about the summertime, but with a recent turn to indoor water and theme parks, and wintertime activities, the off-season tourism has more than quadrupled in the several years. Even still, many of the attractions and even hotels operate on a seasonal basis, from about April – September (outdoor waterparks open later and close earlier). Seasonal attractions, when appropriate, are noted in the listings.

What is "Family Friendly"?

Everybody has his or her own rules and guidelines for what is (and is not) appropriate for his or her children. Wisconsin Dells has lots of great family attractions, and this book mentions those attractions that have a "family friendly" attitude. *However*, this does *not* guarantee that the attraction meets any kind of standards for you or your family. It is merely an opinion that the attraction tends to be acceptable to some families as being appropriate for children. You are urged to contact all establishments directly to avoid possibly exposing your children to something inappropriate.

What contact information is available for the attractions listed?

When readily available, contact information is listed for the attractions. Websites, addresses, and phone numbers are generally listed with the item. If there is no contact information, refer to the section or chapter heading, which may have additional contact information. If all else fails, check the "Research" section at the back of this book.

What about Internet Resources?
The Internet is a beautiful resource as a collection of all human knowledge. Research for this book has relied heavily on information available on the Internet. However, because of the constantly-changing and oftentimes inaccurate information contained therein, the facts here have verified with multiple internet sources, both on "official" websites (sites owned by the company itself) or third-party collections of information (such as online travel guides). When applicable, the official websites are listed in this book, so readers may obtain additional information provided by these sites. Of course, *the accuracy of all websites listed here are not guaranteed.*

To access the web sites listed here, use any of the more recent and popular web browsers. Use the standard website address format:

http://www.*websitename*.com

unless listed otherwise (to save space, sometimes the prefix "http://www." may have been omitted from a listing.

How to Use this Book

Items are listed within subject groups. Based on information availability, the attraction may have an address, website (🖱), and/or telephone number (☎). Some items have other items within them (for example, a restaurant within a casino). In this case, the contact information may be with the inline text, or there may be no contact information. Sometimes, items may be listed in multiple sections or one place inline and another place as a full entry. Such treatment is the author's choice, based in part on coverage need.

Attractions *do not* have specific directions on how to get there, other than their general area (Wisconsin Dells Parkway, Lake Delton, Baraboo, etc). Please contact the attraction directly or refer to maps for this information.

Headlining must-see attractions are designated with the 🏆 symbol. The author made these and all other qualitative value judgments.

Chapter Title

SECTION TITLE

ITEM NAME
ADDRESS
☎   Phone Number
🖱   Website
Item description and review.

Sample Chapter Listing

The American Vacation

Contents:
Tourist Towns
Where to Go
When to Go
Destination Research
Planning Finances
Packing
How to Get There
Where to Stay
Where to Eat

This section provides a general overview of American vacation destinations. It answers some general questions ("where and when should I go?") and some more specific questions ("how much should I tip?"). It is intended to be a general guide to vacationing in America, and not specific to any particular town or time.

Please note that all information in this section is subjective, based mainly on personal experience. Some people prefer airplanes, some prefer to drive. Some prefer large resorts, some love small ones. Use this information as a general guide only; your actual vacation choices are personal and reflective of your own sense of fun and adventure.

TOURIST TOWNS

It is that one thing which draws us there. It is everything else that keeps us there.

It always starts with just that one thing. It could be a large waterfall on a river connecting major commercial ports. It could be a unique rock formation, present in only a few places on earth. Maybe it is a special mountain range with a unique shape. It could even be a beach, singled out by its proximity to a major urban area. Many times, this one thing has occurred naturally, created by time; occasionally, however, it is a fabricated concoction of money and imagination. Whatever it might be, that one thing attracts visitors: many, many visitors. Thus, the seeds have been planted for a tourist town.

It takes the insight of just one person to discover the potential of a built-in base of regular visitors, trekking across the country to visit that one thing. Once discovered, others follow, until the town blooms with activity and commerce centered on entertainment and tourism. This is the story of the American Tourist Town. From the East Coast to the West Coast, from North to South, these towns bring in much of their income through tourism.

What are those "one things" which brought the first tourists? It all depends on the town. Atlantic City, unofficially America's first tourist town, is the closest ocean point to Philadelphia, so the easy ocean access brought wealthy vacationers as early as the late 1700s.

Las Vegas, one of the latest bloomers and arguably the most famous American vacation destination, did not get its real start until the 1940s. It is a largely man-made destination in an otherwise unimpressive desert oasis, where vacationers come not to see the desert, but to enjoy the fruits of ingenious labor.

And then there's Orlando. As ingenuity brought visitors to the desert of Nevada, so ingenuity also brought visitors to the swamps of Florida. This once small town and its surrounding lands have become the number one vacation destination in America, with theme parks, massive resorts and hotels, countless small attractions, and of course, warm weather year-round.

Whether or not these places are tourist towns or "tourist traps" is a distinction best left to the tourist. But for millions upon millions of vacation-lovers, the American tourist town has proven overwhelmingly successful.

WHERE TO GO

The United States is huge. As the third largest country in the world (in terms of land space, behind Russia and Canada), there appears to be enough space to house a seemingly unlimited variety of vacation possibilities. Surprisingly, however, much of it (both that which is natural and that which is man-made) is largely the same. Although major cities, communities, and destinations all have their own special "something" that make it stand out, an American City is an American City, no matter how you look at it. What differentiates one destination from the next is a colorful combination of geography, local laws, corporate interaction, history, and primary trade.

Each sector of the United States has its own unique features. They each have their big cities, their tourist towns, their relaxing getaways and their commercial hubs. For simplicity, these sectors can be divided, roughly from east to west, as follows:

THE NORTHEAST

Arguably the commercial, economic, and cultural center of the United States (and – some would say – the world) is the Northeast. After all, our nation was founded by early European settlements in the area, and as such these cities have had time to grow into massive sprawling mega-centers of everything.

Of course, New York City – America's largest city – is the real powerhouse. Boston and Washington, D.C. are here too. Atlantic City, Williamsburg, Niagara Falls, the Adirondacks and the Pocono Mountains are packed within one of the most densely populated areas of the continent.

THE SOUTHEAST

Thanks primarily to Walt Disney World, Orlando, Florida is the number one vacation destination in America. It has around 40 million visitors a year, surpassing even New York City. Walt Disney World has almost become a rite of passage for American families. If you have a family, you take them on a Disney vacation.

But, for the American vacation, the Southeast doesn't have to end with Orlando. Myrtle Beach, the third most visited city on the east coast (behind New York City and Atlantic City) is a kitschy beach-and-golf-lovers paradise. Pigeon Forge and Gatlinburg are two other major hubs of tourism in the South.

THE MIDWEST

America's most expansive section is the Midwest. From the large flat Great Plains of the Dakotas and Montana to one of the country's most beautiful cities, Chicago, here the quintessential images of Americana are on display. Roadways and railways connect cities and towns, with enough open air to grow for many, many years to come.

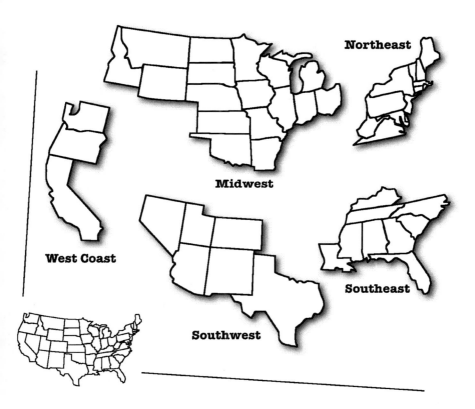

Northeast

Midwest

West Coast

Southeast

Southwest

The Midwest's unique brand of tourist spots has given meaning to "roadside kitsch". As travelers make their way from the East to the West coast, a slew of possibilities are passed. Among these, Brainerd is among the most folkloric. Wisconsin Dells, Branson, the Ozark Mountains, and even Jackson Hole attract visitors to the West's expansive parklands and spectacular natural monuments.

THE SOUTHWEST

The American Desert has more than its own share of oases scattered around the rocky, dry landscape. Las Vegas is the prime example of this – a city built on *nothing* but raw ambition (and billions of corporate dollars). Much of Nevada's reliance on legalized gambling to attract tourist dollars can be seen in the development of several other vacation-centered towns in the state.

THE WEST COAST

California is virtually one non-stop tourist town, which can be looked at as both a blessing and a curse. It is the nation's most populous state. Los Angeles is the original tinsel-town. It has a cornucopia of fun possibilities, both in the city itself and for many miles around it. Yosemite National Park is one of the most visited of all the national parks. San Francisco's rich culture and spectacular scenery make it a must-see. Further north, Washington State and Oregon are the great Pacific Northwest, home of some of America's greatest natural beauty.

WHEN TO GO

Timing is not everything, but it sure can account for a lot. Sometimes vacation times are planned based on school days, holidays, and availability of the party involved. Other times, vacations are scheduled according to the season. As a rule of thumb, the more people that have the day off, the more likely your destination will be busy. Following is a general breakdown of the annual "vacation periods" and off-season times.

SUMMERTIME

When schools are closed and the weather is warm, vacations are obviously popular. Although summer (May through August) is always busy, the days surrounding Independence Day (July 4) is the second-biggest vacation period of the year, surpassed only by the week between Christmas and New Year's Day.

OFF-SEASON AND WINTER

Different destinations have different "off-seasons" (time when attendance is lowest). In general, however, there are two off-season periods: the time right after the holiday season (January and February), and the time just after the summer (September and October).

Despite having fewer attractions available off-season and in winter, keep in mind that this is one of the most affordable and easiest times to vacation (as long as it's not based on skiing or any other winter activity). Hotels are cheaper, crowds are far smaller, and many times it may not even matter that it's blisteringly cold outside, if the attractions are indoors. The trouble with off-season, of course, is that fewer people have availability to travel during these times.

HOLIDAY SEASON

The "holiday season" refers very generally to the time between Thanksgiving and New Year's Day. During this time, when many schools and businesses have vacation, it is by far the busiest vacation time of the year. Flights are booked, and hotel rooms and attractions are the most expensive and crowded. Yet this time of year is often the only time that families and friends have off to enjoy a vacation.

Because of the high influx of tourists (particularly in the warmer climates), vacationing during this time means resorts and attractions are up and running in full swing, special events are common, and crowds are unavoidable. It is the vacation season in America; enjoy it if you like the festive crowds. If not, consider an alternate time.

WINTERTIME

Keep in mind that cold-based vacations (snow skiing, etc.) will *not necessarily* keep a different schedule, though winter activities are of course not available during the heat of the summer. The season may just be shorter.

DESTINATION RESEARCH

The more you know about your chosen vacation destination, the more you can do, and the more fun you'll have. Whenever possible, take care to learn about an area's history, culture, and any specific landmarks and attractions that pique your interest. Not only will you better appreciate your time there, the anticipation of seeing the sights will be that much greater.

CHAMBER OF COMMERCE

Most cities in America have a Chamber of Commerce. This publicly-funded organization (generally a branch of the local government) seeks to promote the city's commercial aspects – stores, tourist attractions, hotels, and such. The chamber will likely have pamphlets and fliers, contact information, and even area maps dedicated to the commerce of the city. Local businesses oftentimes rely heavily on the promotional services that the chamber provides.

VISITOR'S BUREAU

For cities with particularly large amounts of commerce generated by tourism, a separate division of the Chamber of Commerce will exist. Called the "Convention & Visitor's Bureau" or "Visitor's Authority" or some other such name, this special branch of the Chamber of Commerce is dedicated to promoting tourism. If it exists, this can be the best resource for finding out about what a city has to offer tourists.

Promotional booklets and fliers containing area information (which are oftentimes full-color and beautifully designed) are funded by the businesses themselves and the Bureau. Therefore, information obtained via these sources is biased, but it still offers up enough information to give visitors a thorough idea of the area's offerings.

INDEPENDENTLY PRINTED TRAVEL GUIDES

With few exceptions, printed travel guides tend to offer a lot more information than the vacationer needs, which may result in overcomplicated vacation planning. Certain high profile destinations such as Las Vegas and Orlando have many books devoted to that specific location. But other locations, such as Niagara Falls and Wisconsin Dells, may only be covered in a section of a much larger book (like those covering "New York State" or "Wisconsin"). These guides may help if you prefer having a broader focus, but don't mind sifting through countless indexes of locations, restaurants, hotels, attractions, etc.

TRAVEL AGENTS

Commercial travel agents make planning vacations a breeze. They can search for the best deals, book flights and hotels, make restaurant reservations, and even make special requests on your behalf. Their most important asset, however, is their personal knowledge of the destination. They can recommend places to stay and things to see and do like no book or website ever could.

However, their service comes with its own price tag, which can be avoided by simply doing your own research – travel agents have no real greater power than a well-informed customer; they just have access to the right information.

THE INTERNET

Travel information constantly changes, and the Internet is a great way to keep up. Unfortunately, because of the largely level playing field of web sites, it is hard to know which sites to trust and which sites to examine with a bit more skepticism.

A definitive Internet source cannot be offered here; the best advice in learning about your destination of choice would be to (1) check multiple internet sources, including promotional sites, online travel agencies, and sites with user comments, and (2) check the "official" site, if any – official, meaning the site owned by the attraction or city you are interested in.

PLANNING FINANCES

Vacations are expensive, but with proper planning and with the right choices, the costs can be managed. For major vacation expenses, credit cards are often the preferred payment method, especially when it comes to keeping and holding reservations.

Vacation costs can be divided into five basic categories: travel fares, accommodation prices, food money, attraction money, and spending money. This section provides an overview for planning each of these.

TRAVEL FARES

Traveling to and around the destination can be the most expensive and unavoidable cost of any vacation. Though you can shop around for the best bargains on plane tickets, rental cars, and/or public transportation, these costs will accumulate and there is not much that can be done, except to hunt for the best deals. Travelocity.com and similar travel sites are very comprehensive when it comes to booking all kinds of transportation options, and allows you to compare itineraries. Fortunately, prices generally do not fluctuate greatly between competing online agencies.

Credit cards are the payment form of choice for most transportation vendors. Advance payment of plane tickets is customary, whereas rental cars prices are not actually charged until the rental is complete.

ACCOMMODATION PRICES

Pricing for accommodations varies widely depending on hotel. If you must save money, you can try finding the cheapest area hotel. However, your choice of accommodation will affect your overall vacation experience, so save wisely. Many people like to splurge on upscale hotels or resorts to add to their vacation experience, whereas others prefer modest accommodations so they have more to spend on the attractions.

In any case, getting good deals on hotel rooms is another matter of simple research. Sometimes, calling the hotel directly will offer the best deals. Otherwise, online travel agents like Hotels.com or Travelocity.com allow more thorough price shopping. You may be required to pay for the first night, or the entire hotel stay, in advance (the rest to be paid upon checkout). Again, credit cards are generally required to hold a room reservation.

FOOD MONEY

Food can be as cheap as five dollars a day to as expensive as hundreds of dollars per meal, depending on what kind of dining experience you want (fast food, room service, fine dining). Eating out is often a highlight of vacations, as eating in is not usually an option. As a result, food expenditures tend to be a major factor in any vacation budget.

ATTRACTION MONEY

Many vacations don't require "admission" or "attraction" prices, but for those that do, these can make major dents in your wallet. Like travel fares, money used for attractions is unavoidable. Admission prices rarely fluctuate other than the occasional "coupon day."

Buying area attraction packages (multiple admissions for one price) sometimes helps, as does purchasing multiple-day admission passes (as long as you plan to actually go those days). Unlike travel fares, shopping around for a good admission price does not help; you can't substitute one attraction for another like you can with airlines, and the fee is generally fixed regardless of outside factors. The one exception is time-share presentations; be wary though, these "tours" can end up costing you much more than the price of the "free" admission ticket you receive.

SPENDING MONEY

Do you plan on buying lots of gifts for yourself, your friends, or your family? If so, or if you plan on making lots of impulse purchases, be sure to partition enough spending money.

PACKING FOR YOUR TRIP

Knowing where to go is one thing, but you'll need to pack the right equipment to have a good time. Remember, pack what you *think* you'll need. A good suitcase isn't only filled with things you know you'll use, but also what you *might* use. This section provides some tips on packing the right items for your vacation. But don't worry; if you do end up forgetting something, chances are you can buy a cheap one at your destination.

PACKING LIGHT VS. PACKING RIGHT

It is an age-old debate: do you bring too much on your trip, or not enough? The answer to this depends entirely on one thing, and one thing only: transportation. If you're just planning on staying in one spot, you don't need to worry about how much you bring, since you only have to lug it to your room once. However, if you will be traveling around, changing hotels, or otherwise require transporting your luggage regularly, you may consider traveling light.

If you pack *very* light, you may be able to avoid checking baggage on an airplane, and instead carry it onboard with you. This eases the strain of navigating the airport baggage claim (and minimizes lost luggage worries). Packing too much, on the other hand, means you may be more prepared for the unexpected.

Of course, what is essential and what is not rests with the individual; if you must bring your lucky hat everywhere you go, and won't have fun without it, then obviously, it is essential!

CHANGES OF CLOTHES

Of course, pack to reflect your destination! If you're going to a warm climate where it rains a lot, pack summer clothes and a rain jacket. If you're going to a colder area, bring winter clothes and warm coats. As a guideline, it's best to follow the basic rule of packing: pack for at least one additional day. If your trip is three nights, bring four changes of clothes. If your trip is longer than a week or so, it may be a good idea to look into laundry facilities nearby (oftentimes in the hotel or resort), since bringing more than a week's worth of clothes may be cumbersome and unnecessary.

TOILETRIES

Toiletry kits are the easiest way to store and manage these basic items. On the upside, basic toiletries are cheap and small and widely accessible, so even if you do forget something, in many cases they might be cheap to replace, or even free – many hotels offer free toiletry items (razors, toothbrushes, etc.) to guests upon request.

MEDICATIONS

Make sure you have all necessary medications with you before leaving home. It is highly recommended that you pack medications the night before you leave, and double/triple check to ensure you have the right medications and enough to cover your trip, plus at least one day to be on the safe side. Also, keep medications close to you at all times (carry onto airplanes, keep nearby in the car, etc.)

TRIP SPECIFICS

Don't forget sunscreen, camera, film and batteries, bathing suit, sunglasses, contact lenses, warm coat, rain jacket, waist pack, purse, long socks, a nice set of clothes (for a nice dinner), packed food for munching, driver's license or photo identification (or passport if you are a non-U.S. citizen), and whatever else your destination may call for.

HOW TO GET THERE

Exploring the United States takes a bit more than a handshake. Although the elaborate system of roads, highways, and railways keeps everything connected, the distances between destinations can be staggering. New York is about 2,750 miles from Los Angeles. As such, it is important to plan how you are going to get to your destination.

FLYING

The nation's many airports make jumping from one end of the country to the other a virtual breeze. For distant destinations, the convenience of flying far outweighs its cost versus driving. For that reason, when traveling to destinations more than a few hundred miles from home, the necessity to fly there is almost an unspoken acceptance.

Commercial American airports fall under two basic categories: **international** and **regional**. International airports tend to have many flights per day departing for more than a few destinations both domestically and internationally. They are generally located near higher population densities such as major cities. International airports feature connecting flights, perhaps multiple terminals and a choice of airline carriers. Regional airports are more common in rural areas, and many times serve to get people into a nearby international airport

to make a connecting flight to their destination.

Depending on your starting point and destination, you may need to transfer several times from regional to international, and maybe back to regional. Additionally, airport accessibility is directly related to where your travel begins. Those living in major urban areas may find that as many as three or four airports are a short ride away. More suburban or rural area travelers may have additional transportation cost and time to reach the nearest airport.

If all this sounds like too much of a headache, relax! Airlines are used to booking flights with multiple connections. By simply picking a starting and ending point, online travel agencies or even the airline itself will automatically choose your route, including stopover cities, departure times, and provide you with all your tickets to board your planes. In fact, oftentimes, flights with multiple stopovers are *less expensive* than a direct flight, especially when a direct flight is offered for your starting and ending ports.

These days, the best way to book a flight is online. By utilizing websites such as Travelocity.com, it is easy to compare flight itineraries, stopover cities, and travel times. Just input the starting and ending points, right down to the street address, and let them calculate everything.

DRIVING

Of course, with an unsurpassed interstate highway system, America is a road junkie's paradise. From trips as short as an hour to as long as four days or more, millions of people are at home on the road. Virtually every location in America is connected with a road, many times as part of a national roadway system.

Most of the major roadways and arteries connecting the continent grew sporadically over the course of many years. However, the introduction of two uniform systems, the U. S. Highway System and the Interstate Highway System, has greatly simplified directional navigation. Instead of road names, roadways have been combined and created with num-

bering systems. The system created an easier means for drivers to find their way around the country. The numbering systems are very specific, with offshoots and alternate roadways meeting specific criteria for any given number, as set by the American Association of State Highway and Transportation Officials (AASHTO).

The **U. S. Highway System** is a collection of roads connecting the contiguous U. S. states in a grid-like numbering system. The roads, for the most part, already existed, but were combined and numbered for convenience. With few exceptions, the road numbers are greater the further west they are located. U.S. Route 1 ("U. S. 1" for short), for example, is along the east coast of the United States.

The **Interstate Highway System** is a series of high-speed limited-access roads. Unlike the U.S. Highways, these roads are wide, multi-lane arteries with almost no stops and limited access throughout the country. The roads were largely designed to be a part of the system, and instead of stopping at intersections, pass under or over them. Interstate 95 (or I-95) travels the general route of U.S. 1 along the east coast.

For road trips, standard trip planning with a ruler and paper map is all but obsolete. Instead, Internet mapping tools such as Mapquest.com help immensely when it comes to plotting out a journey. They can tell you exact distances, route names and numbers, exits, even rest stops along the way. Electronic Global navigation systems are also available, and can show you exactly where you are located.

WHERE TO STAY

While getting to your destination can be an aggravating hassle through the nation's transportation systems, choosing your accommodations at your destination is where the fun really begins! Sometimes the hotel may just be a place to sleep and relax, but other times – such as with a resort complex – it can be the entire vacation experience. Where you stay on your trip is *very* important; it will largely define your vacation experience.

There are no black-and-white distinctions between hotels, motels and resort complexes; many times places will call themselves one thing when they are really something else. However, there are general similarities between these three types of accommodations, which are outlined in this section.

BASIC HOTEL AMENITIES

As a whole, American hotels are the best in the world. They are the largest, the cleanest, and – perhaps most importantly – the most reliable. Hotel chains dominate the industry and set standards for themselves, but independently-run places are still popular.

Regardless of hotel, most of them will have the following basic amenities: at least 200 square feet of private space, 2 double beds or 1 king-sized bed, a private bathroom, toilet, shower/bathtub, television, cabinets and closets, alarm clock, and a telephone with long distance service. In certain places, showers and bathrooms may be communal ("down the hall" from your room). However, this is a very rare occurrence, and almost non-existent with chains.

Hotels range in size from only a dozen rooms or so to as many as several thousand, some have elaborate attractions and restaurants on the premises, whereas others are small with only basic amenities. The range of accommodation in the American hotel is almost as vast as the landscapes they populate.

BED & BREAKFASTS

Fundamentally, a Bed & Breakfast provides travelers with both a room and breakfast for one cost. In actuality, though, these are privately-owned houses where the owners have decided to rent out their rooms for one or more nights. Like a regular hotel, they generally offer private accommodations with all the standard hotel amenities. Unlike a hotel, however, they provide extremely personal and intimate service; you are in a sense being invited to stay in the house of a friend.

Although the quality these establishments vary greatly, they are generally regarded as an expensive but highly personalized and luxurious way to travel. And, naturally, you will be served a home-made breakfast in the morning.

MOTELS

The backbone of the classic American road trip is the motel. Short for "motor hotel," these are small establishments originally designed for the driving trip. Today, these accommodations have become ideal for the budget-minded traveler looking for a private, inexpensive room.

At motels, the guest room count is generally less than 50 (and oftentimes as few as 10 rooms, or even less). They are generally three or less stories high. However, the tell-tale sign of a motel is that the individual guest rooms open up to the outside — hence, guests drive their cars right up to the front door of their room.

Motels are generally inexpensive, and have basic amenities but few frills. Most won't have food available on the premises; some might have a swimming pool. Expect the motel to have smaller rooms and louder ambience.

HOSTELS

A hostel offers similar amenities as a hotel or motel, but with one key difference: the rooms are not necessarily private. A hostel is more of a community rooming situation, like dormitories. In return, these accommodations are among the cheapest possible, with almost no exceptions.

Hostels are popular domestically and internationally, and are known as one of the most inexpensive accommodation options available. Used regularly by young singles and traveling friends, they require a bit more aggression on the part of the traveler than most other kinds of accommodations, but for the budget-minded, they are near impossible to beat.

RESORTS

The king of the crop, a resort is a hotel designed to be an all-encompassing destination. The label "resort" is self-applied, so there is no hard and fast rule, but the idea is simple: it should be an entire destination, where visitors need not leave the premises for the duration of the vacation. With this come several assumptions: there should be restaurants, attractions, shopping, spa services and other diversions, all in one location.

The best-known resorts are always huge; the largest has a whopping 25,000 guest rooms, but any resort over 2,000 rooms is going to have more than enough attractions to satisfy many different tastes.

WHERE TO EAT

For many vacationers, eating is the highlight of their trip. For others, however, it is merely a short break from whatever the real attraction is. There are almost always several different dining choices; sometimes even within the hotel itself.

FAST FOOD

The quickest, cheapest, and generally least healthy way to eat is with fast food. There are so many fast food choices along highways, in cities and towns both small and large. Some of them are drive-through, some are eat-in, but they all offer the same thing: cheap food fast.

BUFFETS

Casino and large resorts commonly have buffet-style restaurants, where all the food is set out in a communal area, and customers are free to just walk up and take whatever they want. These are all-you-can-eat for one price places, with drinks costing extra.

CASUAL DINING

Table service at its most inexpensive and convenient casual dining choices exists in many different shapes and sizes. Appetizer, entrees, snacks and desserts are often offered. Dress is casual, though individual establishments may have their own requirements. Dining at a casual restaurant may take an hour or more.

FINE DINING

Upscale restaurants generally have a finer ambience, more of a dress code, with better food and better service. Enjoying a fine dining restaurant can take several hours, because at these places, the ambience and service is as important as the food.

TIPPING

Restaurant servers, bartenders, and the rest of the staff work largely on tips given by customers. As such, their wage is substantially lower than other occupations.

At a full service restaurant, fifteen to twenty percent (15-20%) of the total bill is a standard tip, which must be divided up between the server, bartender, and bus-person. Tipping of the host or maitre 'd is optional, depending on any special requests made (birthday cakes, special seating, etc.). Tipping at buffets is generally five to ten percent (5-10%), depending on the amount of work that is done by the server.

Why Visit Wisconsin Dells?

South-central Wisconsin is indeed an odd place to find such a tourist haven. There are no massive waterfalls, no oceanfront, and no vast mountain range. Instead there are farms and small communities with a rich history of agriculture. Wisconsin's capital, Madison, has its own set of attractions. But Wisconsin Dells is 50 miles away from Madison, smack-dab in the middle of farm country. What here, in this seemingly random part of the Midwest, could possibly attract millions upon millions of fun-loving tourists year after year?

The answer to this question lies on a small five-mile stretch of the Wisconsin River, with a few funny-looking rock formations mistakenly called "Dells". It all began with these unusual Dells, and from humble beginnings this quaint little nature-loving community became the *number one family vacation destination* in the entire Midwest.

THE DELLS OF THE WISCONSIN RIVER

The Wisconsin River flows about 430 miles, from the forests of northern Wisconsin (near Michigan's Upper Peninsula) to the Mississippi River. Because the river has been historically notorious for flooding, along its uneven path there are 21 reservoirs, and 25 hydroelectric plants, which control the river flow and water level. The river flows past towns and through wilderness, creates plentiful recreational opportunities and preserves wildlife. It is the largest river in Wisconsin, a state with a ballpark of 200+ rivers and tributaries. But the true beauty of the Wisconsin River lies in a short five-mile stretch around the river's midpoint – it is here where the Dells are located.

In generic geographic terms, a "dell" is simply a small valley. The Dells of the Wisconsin River was first called the "dalles" (having to do with stone work) by French explorers in the 1700s, and the Anglican (bastardized) name stuck. While this may be able to describe a great number of similar landforms, it does not bring to mind an image of the Dells of the Wisconsin River. Here, steep rocky cliffs as high as 100 feet border the famous five-mile stretch of water over the water's surface.

There are cliffs, steep cave-like paths, and islands jutting sharply out of the river. These rocks, which appear to be layered, like sheets, on top of each other, are actually an alteration of soft and hard rock; many times soft enough to crumble with bare hands. The formations are as fragile as they are beautiful.

Additionally, the Dells is me to many unique plant and animal species including oak and pine trees that rarely appear together in nature. The extremely rare cliff cudweed and certain kinds of dragonflies and birds can also be found in the area.

Because of the extremely fragile and unique ecosystem, the cliffs and much of the surrounding ecology became a State Natural Area in 1994 and thus are off-limits. However, this does not preclude viewing of these unique landscape features from the Wisconsin River – certain tour companies are allowed to bring visitors into the Dells, generally by boat.

In short, the Dells are a unique rock formation found along this particular stretch of the Wisconsin River. So the "Wisconsin Dells" is both a geological phenomenon and a town named after it.

HISTORY OF THE DELLS

There are many parts to the history of the Wisconsin Dells, from geological to commercial.

FORMATION OF THE DELLS

The rocks that make up the Dells of the Wisconsin River were formed millions of years ago. But it was a much more recent, single catastrophic event that exposed these rocks as we know them today.

About 500 million years ago, part of central Wisconsin was at the edge of a shallow body of sandy water. The sand along the beach was eroding naturally, and over time the weight of the water and sand would compress, and mix with the water to create hard material. The odd intervals of soft and hard rock, indicative of the change in water levels and various natural geological events, created a layering effect. For millions of years, these rocks stood dormant, compressing onto themselves year after year, century after century, eon after eon.

Millions of years later (about 19,000-15,000 years ago), during the most recent glacial Ice Age, much of what is today the United States and Canada was covered by massive ice sheets. However, much of Wisconsin, as well as parts of Iowa, Illinois, and Minnesota (about 20,000 square miles in total), was a "driftless zone" – a place where the glaciers did not touch. As a result, this area has a more rugged landscape as opposed to the largely flat surrounding area. The Dells were on the far eastern edge of this driftless zone. This lucky position possibly preserved the rock formations from being destroyed by the glacier. They were intact, but they were underground.

About 15,000 years ago, as the glacier was melting, it formed many glacial lakes, one of which was massive Glacial Lake Wisconsin, located by the driftless zone. The water filled up and the ice weakened, eventually causing an ice dam to burst and a surge of water to power itself through the region – it cut through massive layers of topography, and exposed the 500-million-year-old Dells. The surge eventually receded, the glacial lake drained, and the Dells of the Wisconsin River were born.

EARLY INHABITANTS – EFFIGY MOUND BUILDERS

Though Wisconsin is known to have been inhabited by Paleo-Indian people during and just after the ice age, specific evidence of Wisconsin Dells' earliest known settlers date back only to about 2,000 years B.C.E. Etchings on rocks throughout the region are some of the principle examples of the earliest cultures, and such petroglyphs and pictographs are common throughout Wisconsin. However, the Dells area had – for a few hundred years – been inhabited by a strange and largely unknown people, about which little information exists; the Effigy Mound Builders.

These were a mysterious people that inhabited the area around 1,000 B.C.E., known today simply as "Effigy Mound Builders." Nothing is known about their culture except that they created earthen mounds scattered around the Dells area. Their culture, it is thought, involved creation of these mounds in the shapes of bears, birds, and other creatures. Once thought to be used for burials (a theory later refuted), hundreds and hundreds of these mounds can be found in and around the Dells, although most of them have been destroyed either by natural or man-initiated means. Subsequent and more well-known cultures have no knowledge of any of these people being their ancestors. So, around 800-500 B.C.E, the Effigy Mound Builders simply vanished without any trace.

The nearby Devil's Lake State Park has preserved (or in some cases re-created) burial mounds left by these people; created between 1,000 and 800 B.C.E. these mounds are all that remain.

NATIVE AMERICANS AND EUROPEAN SETTLEMENTS

Long before western civilization had begun bargaining for slices of the New World, many Indian tribes inhabited Wisconsin, including the Sioux, Kickapoo, and Ho-Chunk (also called Winnebago). The Ho-Chunk was one of Wisconsin's largest tribes, with over seven million acres of space dedicated to their settlements.

In 1635, Jean Nicolet of France was the first European to explore the region and make contact with the various Native American people. At this time the French had claimed Wisconsin, and had lost it to the British during the French and Indian War.

By the 1820s, the United States began expanding west through the continent, and imposing various restrictions on the Native American settlements. British rule was overturned and the U.S. gained its control over the land. Wisconsin was the 30th state to enter the union on May 29, 1848.

The Ho-Chunk (meaning "People of the Big Voice") had been mistakenly called the "Winnebago" tribe. However, in 1994, the Ho-Chunk declared its political presence in western civilization by becoming the Ho-Chunk Sovereign Nation. Today the Ho-Chunk is still one of the area's largest tribes, and they play an active cultural role in the Dells area, even though they occupy only about 2,000 acres – a mere fraction of the seven million acres just a few generations ago.

KILBOURN CITY

Though the surrounding region had been explored since the mid-1600s, it wasn't until French Explorers nearly a hundred years later came to the land that any Westerner officially referred to it by name.

The explorers used the Dells as a reference point during their early surveying. On maps, they make references to "Dalles," a word that roughly translates to having to do with masonry or stonework. It made a good reference because the surrounding landscape was largely similar, particularly to the south and east. Thus, the Wisconsin Dells became one of the first cities to be noted on any map of the Great Lakes region. "Dalles" eventually became the bastardized "Dells," which as an English term means "small valley."

As the population of Wisconsin and the Dells area grew, and people made their way westward, trains began popping up all over the Midwest. The first train arrived in the Dells area in 1857; it ran a crucial stretch of track because it was the point at which the train crossed the Wisconsin River. As a result, a small community began to form.

In honor of Byron Kilbourn, a major railroad pioneer and a chief force in bringing trains through Wisconsin, this new set-tlement was dubbed "Kilbourn City." However, locals and travelers still continued to call the area by the name used by the French. So eventually, in 1931, the name of the city was officially changed to Wisconsin Dells.

DUCKS

The common term for a special kind of vehicle that can travel on both land and water, "ducks" were originally used for army transportation. Today, however, Wisconsin Dells is home to the largest fleet of tour ducks in the world, bringing visitors through the scenic wonders of the Dells and Wisconsin River.

In 1942, in the midst of World War II, a new military vehicle made its way off the General Motors assembly line. The military gave these vehicles the official name D.U.K.W., as they were made in 1942 (D), were an aquatic utilitarian device (U), and have front/all-wheel drive (K) with rear-wheel control (W). Its primary function was the ability to travel on both land and water. General Motors produced over 20,000 ducks during the few years of production (1942-1945), at a whopping cost of $10,000 each. When placed into military use, they were given the informal name "duck" used by troops.

Ducks were used in several capacities during the course of American interests in the war, but mainly to deliver people and goods on water to hard-to-reach ports. One of their most famous uses was on June 6, 1944, when 2,000 ducks landed on the beaches of Normandy for the D-Day invasion. Ducks were also used during conflicts in the Pacific Ocean during the war, as it was one of the only vehicles that could maneuver over coral reefs. After the war, the ducks were largely decommissioned and most retired in warehouses and dumps.

Soon after, they became somewhat of a collector's item. People would acquire, fix up, and re-sell these ducks to interested parties. One such man brought ducks to the Wisconsin River in the 1940s-1950s in order to give tours of the unusual scenery. Today it is estimated that there are only about 300 operational ducks. Many of these are in the hands of private collectors. For public enjoyment, several destinations, such as Seattle and Boston, have duck tours (those with waterscapes), but none as extensive as in the Dells.

DETOUR: MYTHOLICAL INHABITANTS ————————

Charles M. Skinner (1852-1907) wrote about folkloric tales of America in a series of shorts compiled as Myths and Legends of Our Own Land. Among the stories, Skinner describes the unusual people that lived around Devil's Lake (now Devil's Lake State Park). Following is an excerpt from this book, detailing the myth of Devil's Lake:

DEVIL'S LAKE
"Any of the noble rivers and secluded lakes of Wisconsin were held in esteem or fear by the northern tribes, and it was the now-forgotten events and superstitions connected with them, not less than the frontier tendency for strong names, that gave a lurid and diabolical nomenclature to parts of this region. Devils, witches, magicians, and manitous were perpetuated, and Indians whose prowess was thought to

be supernatural left dim records of themselves here and there—as near the dells of the Wisconsin, where a chasm fifty feet wide is shown as the ravine leaped by chief Black Hawk when flying from the whites. Devil's Lake was the home of a manitou who does not seem to have been a particularly evil genius, though he had unusual power. The lake fills what is locally regarded as the crater of an extinct volcano, and the coldness and purity kept by the water, in spite of its lacking visible inlets or outlets, was one cause for thinking it uncanny.

"This manitou piled the heavy blocks of Devil's Door-Way and set up Black Monument and the Pedestalled Bowlder as thrones where he might sit and view the landscape by day—for the Indians appreciated the beautiful in nature and supposed their gods did, too—while at night he could watch the dance of the frost spirits, the aurora borealis. Cleft Rock was sundered by one of his darts aimed at an offending Indian, who owed his life to the manitou's bad aim. The Sacrifice Stone is shown where, at another time, a girl was immolated to appease his anger. Cleopatra's Needle, as it is now called, is the body of an ancient chief, who was turned into stone as a punishment for prying into the mysteries of the lake, a stone on East Mountain being the remains of a squaw who had similarly offended. On the St. Croix the Devil's Chair is pointed out where he sat in state. He had his play spells, too, as you may guess when you see his toboggan slide in Weber Canon, Utah, while Cinnabar Mountain, in the Yellowstone country, he scorched red as he coasted down.

"The hunter wandering through this Wisconsin wilderness paused when he came within sight of the lake, for all game within its precincts was in the manitou's protection; not a fish might be taken, and not even a drop of water could be dipped to cool the lips of the traveller. So strong was this fear of giving offence to the manitou that Indians who were dying of wounds or illness, and were longing for a swallow of water, would refuse to profane the lake by touching their lips to it."

FAMOUS RESIDENTS

Despite its unique rock formations, the City of Wisconsin Dells might well have been relegated to being just another sleepy Midwestern town. However, it was a combination of two pioneering people – H. H. Bennett and Tommy Bartlett – who gave the Dells the kick it needed to cause a boom in tourism.

H. H. BENNETT

Born in Canada in 1843, Henry Hamilton Bennett would eventually hold a career as a landscape photographer. However, long before that, in 1858, he moved with his family to Kilbourn City where he worked as a carpenter. In 1861 he was enlisted for battle in the Civil War, where he was critically injured. When he returned home, he was not able to continue his career as a carpenter.

Instead, he decided to open up a portrait studio, as his uncle was a photographer. The demand for portrait photography was limited, so he decided instead to take pictures of the Dells natural landscape to perhaps attract tourism. He became interested in producing stereoscopic photographs (two nearly identical photographs that, when viewed properly, appear three dimentional) in about 1861, and would show or sell them to travel agents.

Bennett's photographs and stereoscopes made him famous, and people would visit his studio to purchase these photos, as well as Native American-themed souvenir products he was selling. He also invented and modified his cameras for different uses. In particular, he developed a stop-action shutter which helped him take pictures of fast-moving objects.

Bennett took many famous pictures of the Dells during his career. However, by far his most famous work is "Leaping the Chasm." Taken in 1886, the photo depicts his son Ashley as he jumps onto Stand Rock. The photo captures Ashley mid-air (hundreds of feet above the ground), and was originally used by Bennett to show off his stop-action shutter. However, the photo became nationally famous, and drew millions of people to the Dells to see the unusual rock.

Almost a hundred years after Bennett's death in 1908, his original studio was turned into a Wisconsin historic site, restored to its original look during the time Bennett died, and opened to tourists.

TOMMY BARTLETT

If H. H. Bennett is responsible for bringing nature-lovers to the Dells, then Tommy Bartlett is responsible for bringing the vacation-lovers!

Tommy Bartlett first became well-known as a radio personality and announcer. Born in Milwaukee, he began his radio career at the age of 13. By the age of 20 he was a regular, announcing soap operas and other shows every day.

But it was the year 1952 in which his career really jumped, both metaphorically and literally. That was the year he began his traveling ski show, the Tommy Bartlett Ski & Jumping Boat Thrill Show. Tommy Bartlett was not trained or raised to be an aquatic lover or show producer – but seeing a water-ski show on television gave him some ideas.

The show began in Chicago and traveled to Wisconsin Dells. The show featured stunt skiing, boating, and other audience-

thrilling and family-friendly acts. After the show, motorists that had driven into town to see the show brought back bumper stickers advertising the show and the Dells. Largely because of these bumper stickers, the crowds would get bigger each year.

Due to the overwhelming and continued success of the show, he was asked for his show to take up permanent residence in Wisconsin Dells, on the shores of Lake Delton. So he did, and to this day the show remains. Tommy also had other tourist-centric endeavors for Wisconsin Dells, including a futuristic robotic science attraction (which is still there today, next to the ski show) and a greyhound racetrack (which is gone).

Throughout the '50s, '60s, and '70s, few families in the Midwest had not heard of Tommy Bartlett or had not even seen a bumper sticker, Dells or otherwise. Wisconsin Dells (and Lake Delton) built up around the Tommy Bartlett show during this time, attempting to benefit from the massive crowds the show was drawing. It was particularly during the '60s and '70s when the Wisconsin Dells of today was being formed.

Tommy Bartlett died in 1998, at the age of 84, about five years after being inducted into the Water-ski Hall of Fame. Ironically, he had only actually water-skied once in his entire life – when he was 70.

WHO VISITS WISCONSIN DELLS

If you run in family circles and live in the Midwest, chances are you or someone you know has been drawn into this ultra-family-friendly destination. There is little to do here that may not be suitable for young ones; and older members of the family will be happy to find that they themselves will enjoy many of the attractions themselves. Plus, the charm of the tourist-centric Dells, as opposed to a monopolistic resort environment where one corporation controls every attraction, is that most facilities here are independently operated.

FAMILIES WITH CHILDREN

Wisconsin Dells is all about the family. It is an inexpensive and accessible alternative to more exotic family destinations (such as Orlando), and in many aspects families may prefer the unique atmosphere of the Dells. There are so many attractions, most of which appeal to kids; it is very easy to spend hundreds of dollars on just admission fees in a single day.

The Tommy Bartlett Thrill Show is the headlining family show of the Dells that can be enjoyed by people of all ages. However, waterparks tend to be the main draw for kids. A trip on a duck or boat may be exciting, but chances are they will just be anxious to get back to a waterpark. Parents may end up sitting around watching their kids conquer the slides, or enjoying the aquatic activities themselves.

COUPLES

While kids and families will enjoy the hustle and bustle of the Wisconsin Dells Parkway and Downtown Dells, couples in search of romantic seclusion will find several options in some of the areas parks and resorts. Wisconsin is known nationwide for its beautiful wilderness, and the Dells area is no exception. There are resorts and campgrounds spread over many acres and miles throughout the area.

Outdoor activities are the name of the game here; small cottages, Midwestern charm, and the peaceful wilderness all add up to the romance of the Dells. Of course, the tours of the Dells of the Wisconsin River, the canyons, and Lake Delton offer their own charms for couples. Romantic places are off the beaten path of the strip, though shopping, dining and more are everywhere.

SINGLES AND FRIENDS

Within "Downtown Dells," there are plenty of bars and restaurants for singles and friends (over 21) to hang out. Waterparks cater to a younger crowd, but the larger ones especially have a smaller but regular clientele of high school and college students. Roller coasters and thrill rides along the Wisconsin Dells Parkway have a high volume of adults frequenting them, and there are several haunted houses and wax museums which prove for a nice – albeit short – diversion.

Unfortunately, Wisconsin Dells is not a place where people tend to vacation alone. With very few exceptions, most activities are best with groups, friends, or family. Singles – over the age of 21 – who are traveling to the Dells like to gamble at the nearby Ho-Chunk Casino. They travel from nearby Madison or the immediate surrounding area.

ORIENTATION

Much of what the Dells has to offer lies along a single strip of land or in the downtown area. All attractions are generally within a few miles or so of each other (sometimes more). The Dells can be thought of as several distinct "areas" that provide certain kinds of entertainment. Most people traveling in the region will visit most or all of these areas during the course of their stay.

WISCONSIN DELLS PARKWAY

Highway 12 through the Dells off I-94 is largely considered the main strip of Wisconsin Dells tourism (though the strip itself actually encompasses two neighboring towns). Called the Wisconsin Dells Parkway through this area, it is generally parallel to the Wisconsin River (though the river itself cannot be seen on much of the strip) and runs through the village of Lake Delton and into Wisconsin Dells. There are two sections of the strip, separated by Lake Delton: the Parkway North and the Parkway South. There are some attractions on Parkway South (en route to Baraboo), but most of the tourist activity is on Parkway North, from Lake Delton to about three miles north, by the dam, across from which is the Downtown Dells.

On the Wisconsin Dells Parkway visitors will find all the waterparks, and most of the resorts and hotels, amusement parks, and thrill rides. The strip was shaped largely by the arrival of the Tommy Bartlett Show in the 1950s; as such, many of the attractions here were built in the '50s, '60s, and '70s – though there have been considerable renovations over the years.

DOWNTOWN DELLS / DELLS RIVER DISTRICT

Just across the river from the Wisconsin Dells Parkway is Broadway Street, the main thoroughfare for the Downtown Dells area. It a short and congested strip of land (less than 2 miles long) that is jam-packed with tourist attractions – much more so than the largely open-aired Wisconsin Dells Parkway.

The major wax museums and haunted houses are located here, as well as many, many gift shops. Visitors many times park their car either on the street or in a nearby lot and just walk along the street, stopping by the candy shops, museums, and restaurants. Almost always crowded, and always enjoyable, Downtown Dells is the place to go when visitors just want to relax and roam. There are no large entertainment facilities in this section of town, like amusement parks or waterparks. Instead, the main attractions are eating and shopping.

LAKE DELTON

Not officially a part of the City of Wisconsin Dells, the village of

Lake Delton is named after the lake it borders, adjacent to the Wisconsin River System. Most tourism in Lake Delton is spill-off from the Wisconsin Dells Parkway. As far as tourism is concerned, Lake Delton blends in with neighboring Wisconsin Dells, and attractions can be located in either of these places and still be part of the Dells.

Unlike the largely quiet five-mile stretch of the Wisconsin River, the lake itself is a major tourist lake; houses line its perimeter, and summertime boating is extremely popular. One corner of the lake is reserved for the Tommy Bartlett Thrill Show.

BARABOO

Though still small (around 11,000 residents), the city of Baraboo has many more residents than Wisconsin Dells and Lake Delton combined. Baraboo is not a major tourist town, and not officially part of the Wisconsin Dells / Lake Delton tourist area.

However, visitors of the Dells frequently make the 15-mile trip south for several major attractions, including the Circus World Museum and the Ho-Chunk Casino. There are other attractions in Baraboo as well, though there is no central tourist hub.

THINGS TO DO IN WISCONSIN DELLS

Wisconsin Dells has basically cornered the family-vacation market for much of the Midwest. It is not overly expensive; it is easily accessible from several major cities, including Chicago. When coming to the Dells, whether or not you're coming with family, there are several major categories of attractions.

SEE THE DELLS' ROCK FORMATIONS

At the heart of every Wisconsin Dells vacation is the natural phenomenon that brought the original tourist here – the Dells themselves. All visitors, even those re-turning year after year, owe it to themselves to at least see the features that made this place so famous. First-time visitors will probably wind up on a duck or boat tour as one of their first attractions; regulars may take one of these tours every few years.

The best (and in most cases only) way to see the Dells is on the Wisconsin River by tour boat. Whether you decide to take a more thrilling duck tour or more informative and relaxing boat tour is up to you; you'll see basically the same rock formations (though different tour companies highlight different aspects and sometimes take you to different places).

GO TO A WATERPARK (OR AMUSEMENT PARK)

It is really very easy in the Dells to find your way to a water attraction, since there are just so, *so* many of them. In addition to the major parks (such as Noah's Ark, Family Land, and Great Wolf Lodge) many of the smaller hotels and motels also have water-related activities.

More recently, because of the somewhat sudden influx of indoor waterpark resorts, even visitors in the wintertime can treat themselves to watery delights. Though most of the parks are opened only during the summer, many parks and resorts have indoor sections open year-round.

There are amusement parks as well. Sometimes they are attached to a waterpark (many times advertising both "wet" and "dry" activities) and sometimes they stand on their own. The types of amusements offered at different facilities are pretty constant, and generally include go-karts, miniature golf, and roller coasters.

GO SHOPPING

Gift and other shops are abundant, especially in the Downtown Dells area. Sweet shops and tee shirt shops are especially popular. In the Downtown area, it is common to simply park one's car and walk along the busy sidewalk. Shopping options are generally open year-round, so wintertime visitors who have missed out on the summer waterparks and amusement parks can always enjoy shopping.

MISCELLANEOUS

One of the great things about the Dells is that many of the attractions, especially the roadside wax-museum-types, don't take up a lot of time to see, and there are many all over the place. Let the area's advertisements (and the information in this book) do their work; see what looks interesting, and try it out!

NATURAL FEATURES

Any river tour of the Dells of the Wisconsin will almost certainly yield a tour guide with interesting names for many of the rock formations to be seen along the journey. They are named for what they look like, such as "Cow in a Milk Bottle" or "Hawk's Beak". A few formations, however, are worthy of note beyond a simple heads-up during a tour. The formations that follow are all accessible (some only via tour). They all have that classic layered "dalles" look that makes the region unique. They are all located either directly on or immediately adjacent to the Wisconsin River.

STAND ROCK

A large vertical rock formation, Stand Rock seems to be balancing, teetering, on a thin pedestal high in the air. It is disconnected from the rest of the rocks by a chasm that is about 5 feet wide at the top. This is by far the most famous single formation in the Dells, made famous by H. H. Bennett and his several photos, particularly of the famous "leap" across the chasm.

The formation is located just off the Wisconsin River, generally not visible from a boat. On an area boat tour (see the section on Boat Tours), visitors are given the opportunity to dock and walk close to the formation. A viewing platform is provided near the formation to stand and take pictures. It is a rather wooded area so the rock itself is somewhat shrouded in trees and branches.

WITCHES GULCH

The Wisconsin Department of Natural Resources has declared many places within the Dells to be off-limits. The rock formations lining the Wisconsin River are much too fragile, and boats are prohibited from venturing too close to them. At Witches Gulch, however, visitors can actually walk into a deep cavern cut through the rock, almost up close and personal with the Dells themselves.

Here, the temperature drops and the daylight diminishes as visitors walk through this deep and narrow ravine, surrounded on both sides by steep Dells cliffs. At some places, the walk is so narrow that it feels like one is deep within a cave. With nothing but a rickety walkway and a few lights here and there, Witches Gulch is definitely a unique experience.

ROCKY ISLANDS

Dotting the Wisconsin River (particularly in the lower section) are out-croppings of rocky islands. Some of them have greenery on top, but they all add to the beauty of the scenery. These tiny islands are visible on several tours, and are made up of the same geologic material that was carved through the Dells all along the stretch.

GETTING THERE

Wisconsin Dells has a central location, making it at once accessible and out of the way of most major U.S. cities. Many people visiting the Dells will drive in from one of the nearby feeder cities.

BY CAR

Interstate 94 is the most direct route to the Dells from most major nearby cities, including Chicago. From Chicago, I-94 cuts through Milwaukee and Madison before entering the Dells region. From the east, I-94 goes as far as Detroit; from the west, it goes up to Minneapolis. Basically follow I-94 and exit anywhere around

Wisconsin Dells / Lake Delton (signage is abundant).

Approximate driving distances to Wisconsin Dells:

Chicago	-	197 miles
Detroit	-	477 miles
Madison	-	57 miles
Milwaukee	-	124 miles
Minneapolis	-	217 miles

BY AIR

The closest popular airport to Wisconsin Dells is the **Dane County Regional Airport** (MSN) in Madison. Milwaukee's **General Mitchell International Airport** (MKE) is more of a drive from the Dells, but it is a larger city with generally more frequent service. At both airports, car rental and shuttle service may be available.

BY TRAIN OR BUS

Greyhound (greyhound.com) has a drop-off/pick-up point just over a mile outside of the Downtown Dells area. **Amtrak** (amtrak.com) customers are also in luck – there is a train station right in the middle of Downtown Dells (at Superior Street and La Crosse Street), making rail access a snap from all over the country. It is serviced by Amtrak's Empire Builder line, which starts at Chicago and runs all the way to the west coast. The amenities at the Wisconsin Dells station are very limited. People traveling directly into the Dells without a car will need to arrange for taxi or rental car service.

GETTING AROUND

Unfortunately, Wisconsin Dells is not a commuter vacation destination like Niagara Falls or Atlantic City. Public transportation in and around the area is extremely limited. Visitors wishing to explore the Dells without a car will either need to stay painfully close to whatever attraction they will spend the most time at (and be willing to walk as much as several miles to more fully explore the strip), or hire a taxi or car service. Attractions are generally not centrally located. This is a driving destination.

However, a few of the resorts (indoor waterpark and casino) offer shuttle service from major points of arrival to their destination, and also to select other destinations around town. If you plan on staying at one resort (which is very possible, since some of the resorts are extremely large and fun-filled) then Wisconsin Dells will make a great car-less trip.

SPENDING THE NIGHT ——————————————————

Enthusiasts of large resort hotels take note: part of Wisconsin Dells' charm is in its small motel-style accommodations. Therefore, large resort complexes are *not* the main attraction here. Sure, there are resorts, but they are not large (a "large" resort in the Dells may still have only 300 or so rooms).   Room prices in the Dells can range from as little as $30 per night at a small motel to hundreds of dollars for a deluxe resort suite.

The charming motels along the strip and in the Dells are the prime locations for the 8,000+ rooms within the area. Still, if it's a resort you're after, Wisconsin Dells has its own special brand.

RESORTS

There are a few larger resorts within the Wisconsin Dells area. The resorts generally have a small number of rooms (perhaps as many as 300), but will probably have lots of on-site amenities. Within the Dells, resorts are centered on indoor waterparks. For visitors wishing to have very easy access to a year-round waterpark, restaurants, stores, and other recreational activities under one roof, consider staying at one of the Dells' few resorts.

MOTELS

There is a thin distinction in the Dells between a hotel and motel; but by far the quaint roadside motel is the top accommodation. Most of them are not chains, but rather operated independently.

Many of them have waterparks, either indoor or outdoor, directly on the premises. In fact, a vast majority of water-related activities within the Dells are not from within a large waterpark, but rather are part of one of these smaller hotels or motels, accessible to guests only. Many of the motels actually call themselves "resorts" because they have an on-site waterpark, but this is a distinction that may otherwise be lost.

Some motels have special attractions, such as a location on a large forested property, complete with log cabins, for a more "rustic" retreat. Others strive for all the comforts of home. In any case, for a true Midwestern Wisconsin Dells experience, staying at an independent motel is definitely the most popular way to go.

CAMPGROUNDS

Commercial campgrounds are popular destinations throughout Wisconsin. In the Dells, "fair-weather camping" is the perfect way for those who don't know whether or not they like to camp – or want to camp in more comfort. Here, the campsites aren't out in the middle of nowhere; many have shower facilities, game rooms, pools, and you can even buy your own firewood from the check-in building or lobby. It's the easiest possible way to camp. You can pitch a tent or rent one; sometimes you can even rent a trailer or rustic cabin. You can basically cater your experience to your needs, depending on how rustic you want to live.

DELLS SEASONS

It should be no surprise that Wisconsin Dells gets most of its visitors in the good ol' summertime, but there are in fact four distinct seasons in the Dells, each of them bringing a unique opportunity for a vacation (Note: temperatures listed are approximate, based on a 3-month season, and measured in Fahrenheit).

SUMMER
Average High: 82 degrees
Average Low: 58 degrees
When the weather is hottest and the days are longest, the Dells are up in full swing. Though the official tourist season runs from about April to about October, the most popular times are in July and August.

Summer visitors experience the Dells' outdoor water and amusement parks and tours, which are the primary seasonal attractions. Hot weather keeps the population of the city thronging with tourists. All resorts are open; all indoor and outdoor waterparks are in full swing and are regularly crowded.

FALL
Average High: 60 degrees
Average Low: 39 degrees
When the crowds from the water and theme parks disperse for the season, the natural beauty of Wisconsin Dells becomes the focus.

As temperature descends and leaves change color, visitors focus more on exploring the Dells by tours (such as boat and duck) or on foot (hiking).

Many summertime attractions are still open during much of the fall season (Noah's Ark Waterpark, for example, runs through much of September), but hours are significantly reduced. The diminished summertime population and lower temperatures allow for a much more peaceful and beautiful atmosphere. Couples and groups without children may prefer travel during the fall.

WINTER

Average High: 30 degrees
Average Low: 10 degrees
Wisconsinians know that winter brings about a special atmosphere in the region; swimsuits give way to snowmobiles, and sandals give way to ski boots. But even though a thick blanket of snow covers nearly everything, the doors of some of the best attractions around are still out in full swing. Of course, winter is the time where indoor waterpark resorts shine! At these places, the water is always warm and oftentimes crowded. Also, many of the shopping and indoor attractions are open year-round, including wax museums and various Downtown Dells activities. And since the summertime river tours are closed, there is much less traffic and congestion.

Winter sporting activities are also abundant. There are many snowmobile and skiing trails (sometimes converted from golf courses) available for the ambitious outdoorsy type. Horseback riding can also be arranged. Of special note is the nearby House on the Rock (for more information, see the "House on the Rock" chapter in this guide), which has special wintertime decorations throughout the attraction.

SPRING

Average High: 60 degrees
Average Low: 34 degrees
Spring is the in-flux time for the Dells. While the winter attractions generally stay open continuously, it generally takes time for the summer attractions to open. Therefore, with few exceptions, spring activity availabilities are often the same as wintertime ones.

River tours are among the first seasonal attractions to open, which have their start around the middle of the springtime. Outdoor waterparks are not yet open so the crowds are still at their lowest.

High school spring break is a very popular week in the Dells, so those wishing to avoid major crowds should plan ahead to skip these often-tumultuous weeks around March and April. Otherwise, before the first days of summer, spring in Wisconsin Dells can be a peaceful and pleasant experience.

Dells Early Photography

As the Dells of Wisconsin was one of the Midwest's first tourist draws at a time when photographic ingenuity was blossoming in the mid 1800s, it was only natural that these new practices were highly utilized to entice visitors to the Dells. Photography was a newer art form, and the Dells was one very prominent canvas. The photographic procedures detailed in this section were not invented here; but the coincidence of the Dells' birth of tourism and the presiding technology made it a happy marriage.

STEREOSCOPIC PHOTOGRAPHY

Stereoscopic photographs, like the one pictured here, were very popular for viewing naturalistic images. Thanks to pioneers such as H. H. Bennett, these types of unique photographs were distributed across the United States, and were especially prevalent with Dells images (the stereo image shown here, called "Boating in the Wisconsin Dells", was published circa 1901 by C. H. Graves).

How they work: using a special stereoscopic viewing device, people would see one image in each eye. Since the two images are slightly offset from each other, the result would be a kind of rudimentary 3D image that gave a surprisingly realistic view. Landscapes and distant objects with a main foreground focus yielded the best results – the further the foreground was from the background (within certain well-studied limitations), the better the image looked. Therefore, the Dells of Wisconsin made a great location for these types of photos, and many thousands were made between 1880 and 1920.

Stereoscopic images were made with a special kind of camera. It had two separate lenses about 2.5 inches away from each other to mimic human eyes. That way, the distance of objects would be offset appropriately; distant objects would be less displaced than the nearer objects, giving depth. The exact same basic principle is used today (based on characteristics of the eye) in the form of 3D glasses for motion pictures.

A fun side-note: it is possible, however a bit painful and stressful on the eyes, to view stereographs in full 3D *without* a viewer. Here's how: holding the image a comfortable arm's length away, cross your eyes until you see a "floating," third image in between the two pictures. If you can get this image to focus on itself (by either adjusting your eyes or distance the photo is from your face), then you will see the image properly. Keep in mind (1) smaller stereographic images are easier to see than larger ones in this manner – the ones reproduced in this book may be easier since they are smaller than actual size, and (2) many people can't do it. Be careful though, it is very eye-strenuous.

PANORAMIC PHOTOGRAPHY ────────────────

A panoramic image is basically a very wide picture, much wider than it is tall. They were one of the earliest commercial uses of newly popularized photographic equipment. They were primarily landscape photographs of cities, the countryside, or anything that could be shot at a great distance (commonly, for example, on a nearby hilltop) and that could be expressed well in a long horizontal image. As with stereoscopic photographs, the Dells of Wisconsin was an obvious choice for scenery. And again, thanks largely to H. H. Bennett, there are thousands of these images from the Dells.

A panoramic image can be created in several ways. In the earliest days of photography, a panoramic image was actually a string of several daguerreotype plates (an early kind of photographic technique) laid out side by side. These plates would be developed onto a single, long photo. The photographer would pivot the camera along a tripod and take individual pictures at specific angles so that, later in the development, the plates would "match up" and create the continuous image.

Much later, panoramic cameras were created that actually pivot automatically along the tripod in one continuous-exposure shot. So, instead of multiple plates being created for later fusion, the shutter would remain open while the camera and film rotated in perfect sync. In early photos, it is oftentimes very easy to tell when a panoramic camera was used, and when the plates were used, as seams between the plates can be apparent. Of course, modern technology allows us to "digitally fuse" still images together to give snapshot photos the appearance of a traditional panoramic camera.

H. H. BENNETT

Much of the early commercial success of Wisconsin Dells can be attributed to one man: Henry Hamilton Bennett. Credited mainly as H. H. Bennett, he fell in love with the region and opened up a small photography shop in Kilbourn City (later re-named Wisconsin Dells). Although his official subject matter is that of landscape photography with some portrait work, many of his photos have an artistic quality that go far beyond simple landscapes. His use of foreground subjects set against deep background gave his photographs a depth that suited well both for standard and stereographic photos (both of which he created prolifically). When one thinks about the cumbersome photographic equipment of the day, the camera set-up, and development process, it is clear that he loved the art, from the thousands upon thousands of photographs taken by him.

Until his death in 1908, he took thousands of Dells pictures, including the famous "Leaping the Chasm" image (discussed later) that most see when visiting the area. He published these photographs and placed them for sale in his studio. The images he captured drew more people to the Dells each year. His pieces were sold mainly direct-toconsumer as souvenirs, and it would not be until much later that they finally would become recognized as true art.

Bennett was also hired occasionally to photograph other scenes in other places, but he always returned to his favorite place for what seemed to be an endless stream of wonder. To this day, despite his great contributions to the medium, he remains largely unknown outside a few limited circles – which is unfortunate, because his collection is vast and his vision is everlasting.

Today, Bennett's photography studio is still an attractive tourist destination in the Downtown Dells area; visitors can view and purchase many images from his vast collection, as well as explore the historical aspects of photography. Equipment, film, and more are on display.

Following is a sampling of Bennett's better-known works, from the vast array of photographs, which feature the Dells of the Wisconsin River. They were all taken by Bennett between about 1880 and 1908.

"LEAPING THE CHASM" AND STAND ROCK

Bennett so loved the camera and was so involved in the art and process that he created numerous inventions to help further the medium. Perhaps the most well-known (and unfortunately a technology which remains largely un-attributed to him) was the stop-action shutter.

With a rubber band-type device (which he called a "snapper"), Bennett could open and close a camera shutter almost instantaneously to capture action without the "ghosting" that would appear with a slower shutter. In this way, he could effectively capture a fast-moving ob-ject. To demonstrate this technology, in 1886 he posed a photograph of his son jumping onto Stand Rock, one of the more unique rock formations in the Dells area. The image shows his son in mid-air and the gorge directly below him. The photo could not have been taken without Bennett's invention.

Compositionally, as with most of Bennett's work, this is largely a landscape photograph. There is little foreground information aside from the brush of a forest. In the middle-ground is Stand Rock (partially behind a tree), an out-jutting rock from which Ashley is seen jumping. In the distant background, seen between Stand Rock and the mainland, is the forever-stretching Wisconsin scenery. While the photo has a clear level of technical achievement, it has become known to metaphorically represent achievement or trial.

Stand Rock was a popular photographic subject for Bennett, which he used from multiple angles and many different types of works. He even repeated the "leap" stunt for his photos many times; even taking pictures of it with a stereographic camera. He also had posed photographs of people sitting atop the rock.

For today's visitors of the Wisconsin Dells, Stand Rock is accessible today as a major draw for the Dells' boat tours, but only via tour. Visitors can even see a trained dog leap across the chasm in honor of Bennett's historic photograph. See the Dells' Boat Tours section for more information.

DRAWING TOURISTS

Bennett had a passion for trying to make the Dells look as good as possible to grab tourism. He made it a personal mission to make the area seem like a wild but safe place to visit. To that end, many of his photos depicted tourists, dressed in formal attire of the day, enjoying the sights of the Dells; many times by boat (because in many places that was the only way to see them). Through caves and around rock formations were popular places for Bennett to pose his photographs and subjects. Studiers of his work will immediately notice that he favored certain locations.

LANDSCAPE PHOTOGRAPHS

Bennett loved the landscape of the Dells and the Wisconsin River, and was never short of any place to shoot his next photograph. Bennett's Dells photos rarely went without some kind of foreground focus, even if it was just the banks of the rocks as they stretch back apparently into infinity.

"Leaping the Chasm" by H. H. Bennett (1886)
Wisconsin Historical Society

"The Narrows, Dells of Wisconsin"

"Jaws of the Wisconsin Dells"

by H. H. Bennett, published about 1900

by H. H. Bennett, published about 1894

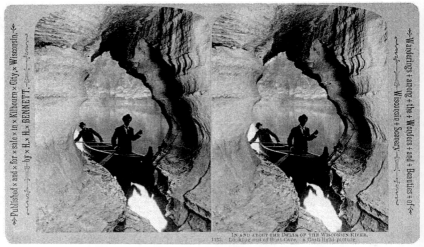

Caption Reads:　　　　In and About the Dells of the Wisconsin River.
1182. Looking out of Boat Cave, a flash light picture.

Caption Reads:　　　　In and About the Dells of the Wisconsin River.
1004. Stand Rock - showing top.

The stereographs on this page have the imprint "Published and for sale in Kilbourn City, Wisconsin. by H. H. BENNETT." They were published between 1875 and 1895. The top photo was published about ten years later than the bottom one.

Inkstand, Lower Dells. By H. H. Bennett. Published about 1900.

Inkstand and Sugar Bowl, Lower Dells. By H. H. Bennett. Published about 1885

Dells Tours

Contents:
Duck & Boat Tours
Other Dells Experiences

First things first. You've come to the Wisconsin Dells; so it is time see these unique natural features up close and personal. And what better way to see the attraction that the city was named after than on a guided tour of the Wisconsin River and surrounding area? Various Wisconsin Dells tour companies offer different tours experiences, including land, water, and a combination thereof.

Unlike Niagara Falls, where the water is a prominent landscape feature, the Wisconsin River is deep in a gorge, largely hidden from the major tourist strips of the area. To fully appreciate these magnificent dells, one can't merely look over the edge; one has to descend into the gorge and travel through the canyon.

Many of these tours divide the Dells into two groups: the **Upper Dells** and the **Lower Dells**. A hydroelectric dam separates the two portions of the river. Both offer similar experiences; some of the tours take visitors partially through the residential areas of Lake Delton, whereas others primarily stay on the Wisconsin River. Of course, the actual path of the tours does vary depending on operating company and mode of transportation.

DUCK & BOAT TOURS

A "duck" is a vehicle that is both a car and a boat. Originally designed for World War II, a duck can drive right off the edge of a road and float into water. While certainly not the only way to see the dells on water and on land, riding in a duck is one of the more unique experiences in the Wisconsin Dells. Of course, there are other places in America to ride one of these unique amphibious army vehicles. Boston, for example, offers similar tours around town and into the Charles River. In the Dells, however, seeing the Wisconsin River in a duck is a must – the ride is bumpy, the "splashdowns" (going from land to water) are intense, but it's a unique enough experience to recommend to anybody visiting this part of Wisconsin. (For more historical information, see the "Ducks" section of this book.)

Duck tours involve a lot of interesting sights; not just the Dells themselves. There are many wooded paths throughout the area that are reserved for these tours only. So visitors can see things on a duck that they just can't see anywhere else. Depending on the tour company, the ducks may enter surprisingly quiet and secluded sections of wilderness only a few short miles away from the bustling center of commerce. They twist and turn through the woods, making their way to the river. When they splashdown, passengers may get a bit wet. From there, they float around the river, eventually making their way back to land. For these tours, ducks carry about 20 passengers each. The entire tour lasts about an hour, and run only during the warm tourist season.

Today, there are two duck companies operating in Wisconsin Dells: the Original Wisconsin Ducks and the Dells Duck Tours. Both are substantially similar, but have some important differences.

Traveling on land and sea with the same vehicle is indeed a unique and thrilling experience. However, for visitors wishing for more of a classic boat tour (less thrill, more peaceful touring), Wisconsin Dells offers several boat tours that traverse both the Upper Dells and the Lower Dells, some with interesting stops along the way.

ORIGINAL WISCONSIN DUCKS

1890 Wisconsin Dells Parkway

☎ 608-254-8751

🖱 wisconsinducktours.com

The Original Wisconsin Ducks has been giving tours of the dells and Wisconsin River for about 60 years. They have the largest fleet of Ducks in the United States – they own about 1/3 of the approximately 300 operational Ducks in the nation. The tour is about 8 miles through the city, the wilderness, and the Wisconsin River. Some of the trails are exclusive to the Original Wisconsin Ducks. This tour operates solely on the Lower Dells portion of the river (south of the dam), and explores many off-road places throughout the journey.

Despite the name, there is nothing inherently "original" about these Ducks. They came from the same World War II mold that the other ducks did, across the United States. They are "original" in that the Ducks were originally used for combat during the war, and have since been refurbished (Ducks are no longer manufactured, and haven't been since the 1950s). Nevertheless, this is one fantastic tour that should not be missed. (Seasonal) ($$)

DELLS ARMY DUCKS

1550 Wisconsin Dells Parkway
☎ 608-254-6080
🖱 dellsducks.com

The Dells Army Ducks is one of several tours offered by Dells Glacial Park Tours. These ducks, which traverse the Lower Dells and Lake Delton, see more of Lake Delton, and more of residential and commercial areas. The Dells Army Ducks offers a small fleet and a rather intimate experience. This tour is ideal for those interested in seeing the more populated areas of Wisconsin Dells; drive around the city streets on a very unique aquatic vehicle.

In addition to the Ducks, the Dells Glacial Park Tours offers a more standard boat tour, the **Mark Twain Upper Dells Tour.** The tour lasts about an

hour on its 15-mile journey. There are no stops on this tour; but the boat pulls up close to many of the famous landmarks while you learn about the history of the Dells. The tour has regular departures during the warm months.

For a more thrilling adventure, also available is the **Wild-Thing Jet Boat Tour.** This wet-and-wild ride is mostly for fun – visitors experience sharp turns, intense speeds, sudden stops, and – of course – the great scenery of the Wisconsin River. (Seasonal ($$)

DELLS BOAT TOURS

107 Broadway
☎ 608-254-8555
🖱 dellsboats.com

Dells Boat Tours, the top-of-the-line
boating excursion company for the Wisconsin Dells, offers a wide range of excursions, with cruises ranging from one hour to several hours, and even dinner cruises and jet boat cruises. Commercial boat tours of the Wisconsin River have been around since about 1856. The tours evolved as new technologies arose: rowboats, gasoline-powered boats, steam-

boats and jet boats. Many tour companies operated until as late as the 1950s and 1960s. Three prominent tour companies, Olsen Boat Company, Riverview Boat Company, and Dells Boat Company, merged to form what is today the Dells Boat Tours. While the Wisconsin Ducks are unique transportation, the thrill of the experience in riding a duck somewhat deters from the genuine beauty of the Wisconsin River. In this respect, the Dells Boat Tours features the best and most comprehensive tours of the Upper and Lower Dells.

The Dells Boat Tours offers several different kinds of tours. However, their two-hour **Upper Dells Tour** is the *best single tour* in the Wisconsin Dells. On this special ride, visitors travel the river and make two very important stops along the way. At these stops, visitors see the most famous features of the Dells: **Witches Gulch** and **Stand Rock**. More importantly, these two features are exclusive to the Dells Boat Tours.

Witches Gulch is a very thin, almost cave-like crevice through the rocks; a mild-temperature path even in the middle of summer. The canyon walls are tall and the air is quiet. Visitors are encouraged to walk freely through the canyon during the boat's short dock time.

Stand Rock, the other stop on the tour has for many years been the symbol of the Wisconsin Dells. It is two "rocks," five feet apart, high above the canyon floor. The famous 1888 picture by photographer H.H. Bennett depicts a man jumping across the chasm. Today, guests of Dells Boat Tours get to stand next Stand Rock and watch, high above, a re-enactment of this famous jump — by a trained dog. This moment is the much-hyped and anticipated climax of an altogether great tour.

The Dells Boat Tours also operates a **Lower Dells Tour**. Lasting only an hour (half the time of the Upper Dells tour), the tour makes no stops, but it does point out many unique features of the Lower Dells, including information about Native American history, various rock formations and glacial information. Both the Upper Dells and Lower Dells tours are interesting, but the Upper Dells is the best. Packages are available to experience both tours.

For those interested in a more romantic boat ride, Dells

Boat Tours also offers a **Sunset Dinner Cruise**. The ride here is about 2.5 hours; visitors are served a full meal while enjoying the twilight of the Wisconsin River, including a nighttime walk through Witches Gulch. Finally, the **Jet Boat** tour offered is an exciting adventure at up to 40 miles per hour of twists and turns along the river. This ride is under an hour, and is designed mostly for the pure thrill of it. (Seasonal) ($$)

AQUA ADVENTURES JET AIRBOATS
W1147 River Bay Road
☎   608-254-7193
🖰   dellsjetairboat.com
A short three-mile drive upriver brings visitors to Lyndon Station, where the Aqua Adventures Jet Airboats make their departures. Designed for very shallow waters (such as swamplands) these unique boats glide across the top of the water, powered by a huge fan which propels them in many directions. Riding in one of these boats feels truly different; visitors glide and swerve with much freedom. Aqua Adventures has three airboats in its fleet. Tour packages vary; they offer Upper Dells tours, thrill-ride tours, "mystery tours," as well as private party options. Tours offered may vary, depending on the season. (Seasonal) ($$/$$$)

ORIGINAL DELLS EXPERIENCE JET BOATS
N422 County Road N
☎   608-254-8246
🖰   dellsjetboats.com
Independently providing tours of the Upper Dells since 1997, Original Dells Experience Jet Boats take visitors (up to 45 per boat) on a 16- mile journey. Visitors get twisted, splashed (sometimes a lot) and sped around the river during the 1.5-hour tour.

A highlight of the trip is Black Hawk Island, a small "dell-formed" island about 8 miles north of the departure point. Here, visitors are taken around the circumference of the island as they look at the various wild creatures (raccoons, deer, turtles, and more) that have made it their home. This is the only boat tour that circles the island – it is not a big island, but its unique shape will be cause for many a clicking camera. (Seasonal) ($$)

OTHER DELLS EXPERIENCES

Following is a list of other Dells-related experiences. See the river, and learn about the history of the region from various points of view.

LOST CANYON TOURS
720 Canyon Road
☎ 608-254-8757
🖰 dells.com/horses

The rock formations of Wisconsin Dells are a unique feature, and Lost Canyon Tours allows visitors to see some of these formations in one of the most unique of ways – by horse-drawn carriage! Daily tours take up to 15 passengers at a time on one of these carriages through Lost Canyon – a deep and dark gorge carved thousands of years ago. Cars and standard transportation do not travel through the narrow walls of this canyon. Though it never gets pitch black, at some places, the light gets so dim, direct sunlight has not touched the rock's surface in many thousands of years.

The tour lasts about half an hour. The canyon is deep and narrow, almost cave-like at times,

and is definitely not recommended for the claustrophobic! Otherwise, this is one of the better tours in Wisconsin Dells. (Seasonal) ($$)

MONSTER TRUCK WORLD
633 Wisconsin Dells Parkway
☎ 608-253-1712
🖰 monstertruckworld.biz

Bumping about in a monster truck can be thrilling, if that is your cup of tea. Monster Truck World packs visitors into one of these gargantuan vehicles specially equipped to handle many riders, and takes you on one of several kinds of rides, ranging from almost calm to car-crunchingly insane. Rides can last anywhere from 3 to 15 minutes. It is one of the bumpiest automobile rides available. Call in advance for off-season schedules. (Seasonal) ($$)

The Parks & Resorts

Contents:
Water & Amusement Parks
Waterpark Resorts

Wisconsin Dells has officially dubbed itself "The Waterpark Capital of the World". Nearly every major attraction and hotel in the area has acquired some kind of water-related activity; whether it be it an indoor or outdoor waterpark or water playground. Additionally, as Wisconsin Dells has historically been a summertime place, to increase tourism during those cold Wisconsin winters, indoor waterparks have been popping up all over the place. Many of them are attached to resorts but some stand on their own.

If Six Flags and Disney are any indication, waterparks and amusement parks oftentimes fit well together. In that manner, waterparks and amusement parks within Wisconsin Dells are merging. Many times there are amusement and theme parks right next to each other, to form more of an all-encompassing vacation destination.

The parks range in size from massive to only slightly more than a swimming pool. The indoor parks tend to be open year-round, whereas the outdoor water and amusement parks are always seasonal.

WATERPARK PRIMER

Waterparks are popular destinations throughout America. Wisconsin Dells, however, holds a unique position this unique world. As the #1 waterpark destination *in the world*, every possible breed of water related activity not only exists here, but it is oftentimes available year round. As such, an entire subculture has evolved devoted to these attractions. At these parks, water can be made to shoot, flow, drizzle, pour and even jump. Basically, if it has to do with having fun with water, chances are it can be found in the Dells, and then some.

It begins with the basic element of every waterpark: a **swimming pool**. Some have shallow ends and deep ends, some have hot or bubbly water, some are for kids and some are for adults, and some even have gentle currents. But they all are all simply man-made holes, filled with water. So what? We've all seen swimming pools. What's so special about them?

Consider making a swimming pool Olympic-size, but less then a foot deep throughout. Then add some small geysers, perhaps a water bucket that dumps hundreds of gallons of water every few minutes, maybe some rope climbs, and squirting cannons. Then decide to make everything (maybe even the ground) out of foam or soft plastic, and design it like a school Jungle Jim, where kids can climb around and get wet in many different ways. This is a **water playground**. These are found in almost every waterpark and water activity center in Wisconsin Dells. They are great places for kids to hang out (with parents, of course!), and a relatively inexpensive way for hotels in the area to claim that precious "resort" status.

But water playgrounds aren't fun for everybody. What about excitement? What about thrills? By adding the second critical element, the **waterslide**, the playground suddenly becomes a bit more interesting. Sure, water

playgrounds have waterslides too; but they are rarely bigger than the standard school dry playground size. No, instead, let's make these waterslides so big that people will have to walk up several flights of stairs to reach the top. Let's make them of a slippery plastic, and lets send a small stream of water constantly running down them, so they keep extra slippery. Lets have them twist around, with steep drops and sharp banks. The slide will end with a splash into a swimming pool. Now let's add several of these slides to the pool, have them twist around each other, and yes, we have the beginnings of a waterpark!

Of course, there are other elements to a true waterpark as well – there are food and refreshment stands, countless lounge chairs, and perhaps the ultimate in waterpark-ness (aside from slides) – the **wave pool**. These are real amusement parks. Spend a hot day at a waterpark. The glossary at the end of this book has additional information about some of the specific waterpark attractions.

WATER & AMUSEMENT PARKS

Following are the major water and theme parks within the Wisconsin Dells. While these parks may have adjoining hotels, they stand proudly and independently, sculpting the Wisconsin Dells Skyline on Highway 12 / Wisconsin Dells Parkway. If you come to the Dells without an interest in glacial carvings, you probably came to visit one or more of the places listed in this section.

NOAH'S ARK WATERPARK

1410 Wisconsin Dells Parkway
☎ 608-254-6351
🖰 noahsarkwaterpark.com

In terms of sheer size and number of activities, Noah's Ark Waterpark sets the bar high on which all other waterparks are measured. With two giant wave pools, over three miles of water slides (requiring five million gallons of chlorinated water), and miniature golf, it is indeed force to reckon with. The "Noah's Ark" theme plays out as animal-themed waterslides and attractions. The park sprawls through a concrete wonderland as an almost random collection of slides and pools, patio bars, playgrounds and so much more. Noah's Ark attracts hundreds of thousands of people each year, yet its regular operating season is only about 100 days long!

Noah's Ark has its humble beginnings in 1979, when the Waterman family purchased a small plot of land to build a simple bumper boat and go-kart track. The next year, a mini-golf course was added as well as the first three waterslides, collectively called **Jungle Rapids**. As the park grew, so did the number of attractions. Throughout the eighties, many more slide complexes were added (including a lazy river), and in 1987 the first wave pool, **The Wave**, was introduced.

In the nineties, focus was shifted more towards thrilling and unique slides, such as **Black Thunder**, an enclosed waterslide with special effects. Park ownership changed in 1994 (to the Gantz family), and more kiddie-type attractions were built. Non-water-based attractions were added as well, such as **Tank Tag**, where people board tanks and shoot each other with soft balls, and **Noah's Incredible Adventure**, which takes visitors through a modern interpretation of Noah and the flood. Today, after more than 25 years of operation, Noah's Ark continues to expand, with at least one new attraction each year. According to the World Waterpark Association, it is America's largest waterpark.

Upon arrival, Noah's Ark Waterpark is deceptively small. The original 205-foot strip on Highway 12 (the Wisconsin Dells Parkway) is all that visitors see when passing the main entrance. It is when they enter the parking lot when they see the size of this mammoth place. The layout of the park is random – there is no central area; the park has been expanding in many cases without the luxury of advance planning. The advantage to this is that the park features many "nooks"; it is very easy to find one of their four thousand lounge chairs, and just relax there all day long. One downfall: due to the millions of gallons of water used, it is unfeasible to keep the water heated to any great degree; smaller parks tend to heat their water more comfortably.

Noah's Ark Waterpark is a clean, family-friendly destination (very popular with even the youngest of children and families) and certainly the best single waterpark in the Wisconsin Dells – a place which knows a thing or two about waterparks. (Seasonal) ($$$)

MT. OLYMPUS WATER & THEME PARK
☎ 608-254-2490
🖰 mtolympusthemepark.com

One of the newest features on the Wiscon-sin Dells skyline is actually the combination of three formerly distinct attractions: Big Chief Go-Kart World, Family Land, and Bay of Dreams. Big Chief featured the coasters, karts, and dry attractions, Family Land was the outdoor waterpark, and Bay of Dreams was the indoor waterpark. Today, they are all known as the Mt. Olympus Water & Theme Park. When combined with the neighboring **Treasure Island Resort**, the 150-acre Mt. Olympus is the largest waterpark resort in America.

And what a visible park this is! As motorists enter the Wisconsin Dells Parkway and drive towards they Downtown Dells, they see in the distance huge twisting roller coasters, and some of the most elaborate go-kart tracks ever created. Surprisingly, the thrown-together nature of this park doesn't seem to show; the different types of attractions fuse together in a way that is rather befitting an eclectic place as the Wisconsin Dells themselves.

The roller coasters go-karts here all have Ancient Greek themes to them. Hades is the world's longest underground 0roller coaster (much of it is under the parking lot). The Trojan Horse go-kart track actually allows drivers to drive through a full-size replica of the fabled horse. The Poseidon go-cart track is partially under water. There is a Zeus and Pegasus coaster, and more.

The Family Land water park is charming, much smaller and more intimate than its colossal water park competitors in the area. Yet there are still the same thrills here, including a nice selection of water slides, a lazy river, and a wave pool. Bay of Dreams is Family Land's year-round indoor water park counterpart, with some nice indoor slides and other aquatic attractions.

Also joining this community is the **Treasure Island** hotel, located next to Family Land and Bay of Dreams. Visitors spending much of their time at Mt. Olympus will greatly benefit from staying here, as they can walk directly to Mt. Olympus attractions. (Bay of Dreams is year-round, the outdoor park is seasonal) ($$$)

RIVERVIEW PARK & WATERWORLD
700 U.S. Highway 12
☎ 608-254-2608
⌂ riverviewpark.com
Located near the busy intersection of highways 13 and 12 (Wisconsin Dells Parkway), Riverview Park & Waterworld is exactly as the name suggests – an amusement park and water park next to the Wisconsin River. The park is small, spread out over 35 acres, but there is indeed much to do within the area.

The waterpark features tube slides, regular slides, a wave pool, high-speed slides, bumper boats, and a collection of kiddie play areas. The amusement park has standard midway attractions, such as go-karts, bumper cars, a roller coaster, and a Tilt-a-Whirl. Tickets are available as a pay-one-price for both the waterpark and amusement park. Guests not wishing to participate (but merely walk around) are not charged admission. (Seasonal) ($$)

TIMBER FALLS ADVENTURE PARK

Highway 13 & Stand Rock Road
☎   608-254-8414
🖱   timberfallspark.com

Around the northern end of the Wisconsin Dells Parkway strip is the Timber Falls Adventure Park – as it is one of the most crowded intersections in the Dells area, it is a hard facility to miss.

Timber Falls began its career as an elaborate mini-golf course called "Timber Falls Adventure Golf." The course is still there, but the park has expanded to include other attractions, including a headlining coaster called Avalanche and a log flume ride called Loggers Lagoon. Also of note at Timber Falls is the "Skyscraper" thrill ride, which flies willing participants high into the air and twirls them about for a few moments – kind of a cross between bungee jumping and a Ferris Wheel.

The park is small, but the attractions are of good quality. Though full-day passes are avail-

able and popular, this is more of a park to spend an afternoon, not a full day. (Seasonal) ($/$$$)

STORYBOOK GARDENS & TIMBAVATI WILDLIFE PARK

1500 Wisconsin Dells Parkway
☎   608-253-2391
🖱   storybookgardens.net

As one of the first non-dells-related tourist attractions in Wisconsin Dells, Storybook Gardens is a familiar centerpiece of the strip. As early as the 1950s, the gardens have been entertaining tourists with its landscape, peaceful walks, and overall laid-back atmosphere. It is a very simple place, where visitors walk around the serene environment and admire the waterfall, ponds, botany (much like a botanical garden) and the various story-book-inspired sites. Among the displays are Simple Simon, Cinderella, Jack and the Beanstalk, and many other classic fairytale characters. The intent is to imitate a classic storybook or fairytale setting. Visitors may also enjoy a train ride around the park, or a carousel ride.

Also at Storybook Gardens is a much newer attraction – the Timbavati Wildlife Park. Integrated well with the garden, this live animal park features all kinds of animals, including tigers, monkeys, zebras, giraffes, and lions. The daily wildlife show, great for young children, allows visitors to get up close and personal with several unique animals. Also available are opportunities to feed animals, pet animals, even ride a camel. Storybook Gardens and Timbavati Wildlife Park are seasonal attractions. (Seasonal) ($)

EXTREME WORLD
1800 Wisconsin Dells Parkway
☎   608-254-4111
✍ extremeworld.com

Extreme World is less an amusement park and more a collection of similarly themed but independently priced attractions. Here, the theme is thrilling and unique attractions that fling visitors around, spin them, and send them freefalling towards the ground. These attractions spring up into the skyline, looking like halfway-completed building scaffolding. Yet when passersby see people swaying about with nothing more than a harness and rope, they realize these are not ordinary metallic adventure attractions.

Get thrilled in several ways: the **Bungee Jump** allows visitors to ride up an elevator and plummet about 130 feet with a bungee chord attached to the ankles. The **Sky Coaster** is like a big swing – lifts the participants up and drops them into a freefall. Then they swing back and forth, at 60+ miles per hour! The **Ejection Seat** pulls back and flings – like a slingshot – hundreds of feet into the air. Or, **Terminal Velocity** basically simulates jumping out of a building – it is a controlled but unattached freefall to a safety net below.

Most of these rides (except for Terminal Velocity) include what they call a "bounce out"; they let whatever contraption you are riding in jostle you around for up to 2 minutes before bringing you back home. For example, the Sky Coaster is allowed to swing back and forth, back and forth, so you can fully enjoy this experience.

Thrills like this don't come cheap – these are expensive attractions, among the most pricey in Wisconsin Dells. Expect to pay $40 or even more per extreme stunt. Extreme World operates seasonally. These descriptions don't do these unusual attractions justice. Visit the attraction's website for more information. Extreme World also has several milder (and less expensive) attractions: a Go-Kart track called the **Super Speedway**, a small haunted house called **Castle of Terror**, and a paintball arcade.

Overall, this is a unique center right in the middle of the strip. Because the rides are all outdoors and exposed, it is especially fun to watch other participant fling into the air as they scream at the top of their lungs. And the best part is, watching them is free! (Seasonal) ($$$/$$$$)

WATERPARK RESORTS

Welcome to the next breed of family vacation destination – the year-round *indoor waterpark resort*. Though it is very easy for a hotel to claim an "indoor waterpark" when they have little more than a standard swimming pool, these facilities can also be massive indoor environments, 45,000 square feet or more of wet and wild fun, complete with waterslides, wave pools, video arcades, lazy rivers, and so much more. Best yet, they are open year-round!

This section details several of the area's waterpark resorts, and specifically notes those which are particularly grand.

"Do I need to stay at the resort to enjoy its waterpark?"

That decision is entirely up to the resort! Some of them will offer day passes whereas others require that only guests of the hotel may use it. With few exceptions, the larger indoor waterpark resorts offer day passes, and the smaller ones do not. Contact the resort in advance for details.

"Water Park? Water Activities? How does one differentiate?"

While the decision is far from arbitrary, what determines the class of aquatic fun (i.e. whether or not the resort houses a full-blown park or just a soup-ed up swimming pool) is in part based on the author's personal reaction to the facilities. Does it have the "feel" of a waterpark? Does it have more then 1 or 2 waterslides and several pools? Are there things to do for adults, older children, and young ones? There are so many levels of variation on what qualifies as an actual water-park, but effort has been made to create a distinction when in many cases there really doesn't need to be.

MAJOR INDOOR WATERPARK RESORTS

These are the cream of the crop. Tourists wishing to experience the true glory of an indoor waterpark resort will likely find their calling at one of these fine places.

GREAT WOLF LODGE
1400 Great Wolf Drive
☎ 800-559-9653
✆ greatwolflodge.com

Already America's largest chain of indoor waterpark resorts, the Great Wolf Lodge has expanded in leaps and bounds over the past several years, since about 2003. There are resorts in Williamsburg, Virginia, Traverse City, Michigan, Kansas City, Kansas, with new resorts on the way across the northeast (including the Pocono Mountains and Niagara Falls). It is clearly a product of Dells commercialism gone national.

The first Great Wolf Lodge opened in the Wisconsin Dells in 2000. This one – the original – is a full-featured resort that has 309 guest rooms (all of which are suites) yet it houses a whopping 65,000 square-foot family entertainment complex. At the top of the list, of course, is the indoor waterpark (open year-round), which features ten waterslides, five pools, a water playground and many more aquatic joys. As this area is almost always teeming with children, there is also an adults-only pool area.

In addition to the indoor waterpark, Great Wolf Lodge features a huge video game center, several on-site restaurants (both sit-down and take-out) an arts and crafts center, a seasonal, smaller outdoor waterpark, and several smaller surprises. Of particular note is the Wiley's Woods complex – four-story interactive "video game." Children and families explore the complex as they solve puzzles, play games of skill and chance, and more, and they earn points.

Great Wolf Lodge is also one of the most expensive hotels in Wisconsin Dells. But it is open year-round, guests play at the park for free, and the appeal of an all-suite hotel (with many levels of suites) makes this one of the finest all-encompassing resort destinations in the area.

KALAHARI RESORTS
1305 Kalahari Drive
☎ 608-254-5466
🖰 kalahariresorts.com

For visitors trekking across America in need of a record-breaking indoor waterpark, they need look no further than the Kalahari Resort in Wisconsin Dells. Here, Africa is the theme and water is the fun! When visitors enter the huge lobby, and wind their way through to the "entertainment" facility, they will find America's largest indoor waterpark. At over 120,000 square feet, this mammoth watery wonderland rivals the size of Las Vegas casino floors. It is simply huge!

The waterpark has more than the traditional waterslides and wave pools (of course it has those too). Two attractions help this resort stand above the rest and let it live up to its reputation. **FlowRider** is an artificial wave designed to simulate ocean surfing. Powerful spray nozzles shoot 50,000 gallons of water each minute up a padded slope to imitate a five-foot "wave." Visitors may they surf or boogieboard it to practice their skills. For the experience, reservations and additional fees are required.

Additionally, **Master Blaster** is unique as well. It is a waterslide that actually propels you upward like a roller coaster! Spray jets push your tub up a 570-foot slope through the course of this very unique ride.

There are two Kalahari Resorts; one in Wisconsin Dells and one in Sandusky, Ohio. The Dells one, however, is the larger of the two. With just over 700 rooms, the resort itself is no small potatoes – and there is more than just the indoor waterpark. The resort features live shows, a seasonal outdoor waterpark, a spa and salon, restaurant and bar facilities, a large convention center and meeting rooms, a large movie theater, a huge video game room, craft areas, and gift shopping. It's a Las Vegas-style resort designed especially for families.

WILDERNESS HOTEL & GOLF RESORT

511 East Adams Street

☎ 800-867-9453

🖑 wildernessresort.com

Just off the main strip (but still very close) is the Wilderness Hotel & Golf Resort. The massive lodge exterior is reminiscent of a grand Northwoods resort. The hotel has been in operation for over 10 years, and is truly one of the great Wisconsin Dells all-encompassing getaways. It has not one, but *four* distinct waterparks (both indoor and outdoor), many on-site restaurants, and even a golf course. The resort is divided into two major sections: the New Frontier and the Wild West. These sections basically divide many of the amenities, rooms, and restaurants.

Aside from these experiences, what really makes the Wilderness Hotel stand out from the rest is its unique accommodations. The hotel boasts about 400 standard rooms – a modest number by any major resort's amount. However, the Wilderness rests on 210 acres of peaceful forest, and within this environment are many

choices of rustic living – log cabins, condominiums, villas, and so much more, each with that rustic feel and theme. These are in addition to the standard hotel-style rooms.

In keeping with the resort's two distinct regions, instead of one larger indoor and outdoor waterpark, the Wilderness has instead divided its wet play lands into four smaller parks, two year-round indoor and two seasonal outdoor. These parks are dispersed evenly between the two parts of the resort – each part has one indoor and one outdoor waterpark.

The two indoor parks are **Klondike Kavern** and **Wild West.** Klondike Kavern, in the New Frontier section, is about 65,000 square feet and features tube slides, a lazy river, a large water playground, a pool, and a dry Laser Tag arena. The Wild West waterpark (in the Wild West section) is an additional 70,000 feet of water activities, including an interactive wave pool and **The Cannonball** – a unique tube ride where visitors spin freely as they ride down a large funnel-shaped slide.

The major wave pool at the Wilderness is unfortunately located outside; hence it's a seasonal attraction. The other outdoor sections, **Lake Wilderness** and **New Frontier**, offer additional 130,000 square feet of slides, pools, and general relaxing space for summertime visitors.

With all these great amenities, the Wilderness might seem like the perfect place to spend a day. However, if you are planning to stay cheaply at a nearby motel and visit the Wilderness' waterparks, think again! These parks are exclusively for hotel guests! This is different from other major resort waterparks (such as Great Wolf Lodge) where visitors may purchase a day pass to the resort's waterpark facilities. At the Wilderness, however, being an overnight guest at the resort is a requirement to partake in the fun.

In addition to the headlining waterparks, the Wilderness is home to the **Wilderness Woods Golf Club**. Unlike guests-only waterparks, the 18-hole championship course is available for day visitors as well (resort guests get a discount). Also on the property are two smaller par 3 courses.

Visitors (particularly children) wishing to take a break from the water or the golfing will be pleased to note the many dry activities available as well, such as laser tag, a large video arcade, and daily activity centers. The resort has many on-site restaurants, ranging from fine dining experiences to cafeteria-style eateries.

What also makes Wilderness appealing is its independence; though it has the feel of a large resort, it is owned primarily by two people and an additional small group of Dells-area investors. In other words, there is no other place like it, anywhere in the world.

POLYNESIAN RESORT HOTEL

857 North Frontage Road
☎ 608-254-2883
✆ dellspolynesian.com

For those visitors wishing to enjoy a complete indoor waterpark resort, but who also do not want the high price tag, many consider the smaller Polynesian Resort Hotel. It has the same basic amenities as the larger indoor waterpark resorts, only on a smaller scale.

The waterpark is divided into an indoor and outdoor section. The indoor section is about 38,000 square feet, and features several waterslides, a lazy river, pools and whirlpools, a water playground, as well as dry attractions, such as a small video arcade. The seasonal outdoor facility encompasses about 4 acres, and has additional waterslides and pools, and an outdoor patio for casual dining.

The Polynesian has been ranked as one of the best waterpark resorts for families with very young children (under age 11) – due in part to its small size and affordable accommodations.

HOTELS WITH WATER ACTIVITIES

It may seem that just about every hotel has some kind of waterpark to call its own (either indoor or outdoor). In addition to the headlining resorts mentioned in the previous section, there are many other, smaller resorts with water activities. While they may not have the wide range of activities to fill an entire "park," these smaller resorts offer a more intimate experience. Following is a list of select resorts with water activities – and in the Dells, this means they definitely have than just a swimming pool.

TREASURE ISLAND
1701 Wisconsin Dells Parkway
☎   608-254-8560
⌂   wisdellstreasureisland.com
Next to the Mt. Olympus Water & Theme Park, Treasure Island offers a great location to some of the best attractions in the Dells. Additionally, the hotel has several video arcades, a private water activity center for hotel guests only, and several on-site restaurants featuring casual dining choices. Of course, the location is all but unbeatable.

COPA CABANA
611 Wisconsin Dells Parkway
☎   608-253-1511
⌂   copacabanaresort.com
With a tropical island resort theme, the Copa Cabana is a difficult resort to miss. Near the southern end of the strip, it is very close to the Tommy Bartlett Show and has facilities located on both sides of the street (it has a connecting walkway). The resort has 130 rooms and suites, and a small indoor and outdoor water activity center. The indoor center, called **Lost Harbor**, is basically a

water playground for young children. Copa Cabana also houses meeting and convention space, and is within walking distance to several nearby restaurants.

ATLANTIS WATERPARK HOTEL

1570 Wisconsin Dells Parkway
☎ 608-253-6606
🖱 dellsfun.com

The Atlantis has less than 100 rooms and suites, and has been given especially high marks (in local publications) for families with children under age 11. There is an outdoor and indoor water activities, with a few small slides in both locations. The indoor facility is 16,000 square feet – consisting of a regular swimming pool and an adjacent water playground.

Perhaps the most enticing feature of Atlantis is its location: it is smack-dab in the middle of the strip, with easy walking access to Noah's Ark Waterpark and Mt. Olympus Water & Theme Park.

RAINTREE RESORT

1435 Wisconsin Dells Parkway
☎ 608-253-4368
🖱 dellsraintree.com

The RainTree resort has about 150 rooms, and is set up for meetings and conferences, with a lounge area. The 22,000-square-foor indoor water activity center at the resort is a nice water playground with a few moderate park-type amenities, such as a medium-sized slide. There is an outdoor pool area here as well.

There is also a dry activity center, consisting mainly of a video arcade. RainTree's location is great as well, right across the street from Noah's Ark Waterpark.

CAMELOT HOTEL & SUITES

1033 Wisconsin Dells Parkway
☎ 608-253-3000
🖱 dellshotels.com

As the name suggests, Camelot Hotel & Suites transports visitors back to the middle ages. Shaped like a small castle, everything here is themed around Camelot and the Arthurian Legend – even the indoor and outdoor water activity centers. Guests are treated to several levels of rooms and suites, an on-site video game room and fitness center, and of course, the indoor and outdoor water areas with small waterslides, a water playground, a whirlpool and regular pool, and a waterfall.

GRAND MARQUIS RESORT HOTEL & SUITES

840 Wisconsin Dells Parkway

☎ 608-254-4843

🖱 grandmarquis-dells.com

Here, guests can enjoy many levels of suites, and a small video arcade center. Grand Marquis has an indoor and outdoor water activity center, both with a small selection of waterslides on the water playgrounds. Aquatic creatures are the theme here.

MEADOWBROOK RESORT

15333 River Road

☎ 608-253-3201

🖱 meadowbrookresort.com

The Meadowbrook Resort is a unique resort within the Dells area. It features just over 30 rooms, but these rooms are spread out in Northwoods-style cabins and lodges over a 12-acre wooded area (some of the cabins are open during the summertime only).

Guests enjoy popular rustic activities such as horseshoe tossing, fishing, tetherball, campfire activities, and bird and wildlife viewing. The 8,000 square-feet of outdoor (and a few indoor) water activities center is small, but the headlining feature at Meadowbrook is the Northwoods-esque adventures.

Animals and Nature

Northern Wisconsin (and the "Northwoods") is the place to which millions of Midwesterners head each year to "get away from it all." All kinds of outdoor sporting and recreation are available in this beautiful and unique part of America. Camping, fishing, snowmobiling,

Contents:
Horseback Riding
Animal Encounters
Boating and Fishing
State Parks

log cabin living, boating, and just plain relaxing are all part of the experience. Wisconsin Dells is not part of the Northwoods, but its centralized location within the state makes it a common gateway for travelers headed in that direction. As such, many of the attractions in the region are reminiscent of the wonders up north, but with less travel time.

A note about permits: some attractions in the Dells area, such as fishing, may require a permit. For information about obtaining permits, and which activities require them, visit the **Wisconsin Department of Natural Resources** web sit e at http://www.dnr.state.wi.us/.

HORSEBACK RIDING

Saddle up and ride 'em, cowboy! There are so many nature trails in the Dells area, and riding through them on horseback is a great way to see the countryside. Although horseback riding naturally requires a certain amount of athletic ability, the stables listed here are for the tourists – no real experience is necessary to enjoy a trot or a gallop, and some of the sites are manufactured (see, for example, an old western town or a Native American camp).

CANYON CREEK RIDING STABLE
60 Hillman Road
☎ 608-253-6942
In nearby Lake Delton, the Canyon Creek Riding Stable mixes adventure, nature, and theme park attraction. This one-hour guided tour takes visitors on horseback through the "old west," including a small western town, the woods, past a river and pond, through a dark tunnel, and even past a cemetery. All this, of

course, is part of a themed experience (since visitors aren't really in the old west). Also on the property is a small petting zoo and wildlife exhibit, which is included with the price of a tour.

Catering to families, the stable operates primarily during tourist season, but may have off-season tours available on special limited occasions. (Seasonal, call ahead for off-season tours) ($$/$$$)

OK CORRAL RIDING STABLE
Highway 16 E.
☎   800-254-2811
🖰   okcorralridingstable.com

Established in 1980, the OK Corral Riding Stable is a slow-paced and friendly saddle riding experience for families. Here, children as young as 5 years old (ability permitting) have been able to ride one of the stables 100+ horses. Open only during the summer tourist season, OK Corral prides itself as having a horseback riding experience more focused on the natural beauty of the Dells. The hour-long guided tours take visitors through the backwoods of Wisconsin, and through the unique "Devil's Canyon" – a sandstone gorge filled with natu-

ral plant life. Also on the tour, riders pass a Native American camp before making their way back to the stable. (Seasonal) ($$)

RED RIDGE RANCH
W4881 Highway 82
☎   608-847-2273
🖰   redridgeranch.com

About 20 miles outside of Wisconsin Dells is the town of Mauston. It is the location of Red Ranch Ridge, a riding stable close enough to the Dells to be accessible, but far enough away that the beauty of horseback riding is not undermined by a major tourist center. Its seclusion is what brings appeal; Red Ridge functions as a true ranch, surrounded by true scenic beauty.

In addition to the hour-long trail rides that show off the surrounding farmlands and countryside, the ranch offers horse "classes" (and day camps mainly for kids), pony rides for the real young ones, and even special events on special occasions, such as Halloween rides. For true equestrians, Red Ridge also serves as a boarding house for horses.

The ranch is open year-round, but visitors should call in advance when planning a visit off-season. In the wintertime, sleigh rides are the prime draw. ($$)

ANIMAL ENCOUNTERS

The rich wildlife heritage of Wisconsin is highlighted in several area attractions that focus on bringing some of these animals up close and personal.

INTERNATIONAL CRANE FOUNDATION
E11376 Shady Lane Road
☎   608-356-9462
🖱 savingcranes.org

Cranes are large birds living in wetland environments. They generally have long legs and necks and are wade in the shallow waters of their environment. At the International Crane Foundation in Baraboo, 100 acres of crane habitat have been either created or restored (wetland, oak savannah, and prairie) to help preserve these birds. Fifteen species of crane call the foundation home, and visitors are allowed to explore the habitat either on self-guided or guided tours. Visitors stay on a pre-defined path through the habitat, and are given helpful information in spotting cranes, and lots of information about these unique birds.

The foundation was established in 1973 to help breed cranes – the tallest birds capable of flying – in captivity before releasing them into the wild. Today, all 15 known species of crane have been successfully bred in captivity, and they continue to be preserved and regularly released into the wild.

The complete tour is both indoors and outdoors, and features various indoor crane exhibits, an art gallery, and restoration information. The International Crane Foundation accepts tours only during the summer tourist season. Guided tours may require advance reservations. The total complex is very large, about 225 acres consisting of exhibits, pens, labs, and tourist areas, so expect a total visit of at least 2 hours. (Seasonal) ($)

88

Wisconsin Dells: A Guide for Tourists

WISCONSIN DEER PARK

583 Wisconsin Dells Parkway
☎ 608-253-2041
Kind of like a large petting zoo, the Wisconsin Deer Park allows visitors to stroll along through a 28-acre forest populated with deer and other kinds of gentle wildlife. Feeding of these animals is allowed and encouraged (with a special feed). Many of the animals are not fenced in; they are free to roam the park, so visitors get an up close and personal encounter. Around since 1952, this is a popular attraction for younger children and their families. (Seasonal) ($/$$)

ALLIGATOR ALLEY

1800 Wisconsin Dells Parkway
☎ 608-253-4800
This indoor exhibit allows visitors to get up close to alligators, and even feed them. As dangerous as this might sound, the alligators are actually kept behind a thick pane of glass, with feeding units every few feet that allow people to place food into them, so they never actually come in contact with these fearsome creatures.

BOATING AND FISHING

Whether on the waters of the Wisconsin River, Lake Delton, or a private pond, there are many diversions for the water-lovers in the Dells that don't involve slides and wave pools.

B & H TROUT FARM

3640 State Road 13
☎ 608-254-7280
🖰 bhtroutfarm.com
Forget about purchasing poles, renting a boat, packing tackle, and cleaning and packing your fish. If you just want to drop a fishing pole into the water and feel the thrill of reeling in a live trout, then the B & Trout Farm will take care of the rest. Established in 1950, they provide poles, bait, a scenic pond stocked with fish, and leave you to do the catching. There is no limit to how much you can fish, and this is not catch-and-release, so you are free to take home what you catch. However, they do charge you by the inch to take home what you catch – not the cheapest way to obtain fish. But it's a lot of fun with not a lot of effort, especially

for families and kids. Plus, visitors may not need a fishing permit. ($/$$)

RIVER'S EDGE RESORT

S1196 Country Road A

☎   608-254-7707

⌗   riversedgeresort.com

River's Edge Resort is a great place for people who want to relax on a boat or fish during their trip to the Wisconsin Dells. The resort features motel-style rooms as well as many levels of rustic log cabins available on a daily or weekly basis. The resort is open year-round.

While also functioning as a full-service motel, one of the on-site amenities available to the public is the River's Edge Boats & Canoes. Visitors may rent any of several kinds of boats, including canoes, pontoons and fishing boats (with or without a motor). Visitors then cast off onto the Wisconsin River or Lake Delton and enjoy a day of boating with whatever their pleasure may be. ($/$$$)

VERTICAL ILLUSIONS

1009 Stand Rock Road

☎   608-253-2500

⌗   verticalillusions.com

Kayak rentals and tours, camping, biking and rock climbing are available at Vertical Illusions, an outdoor recreation outfitter. Visitors can take watercraft up and down the Upper Dells area (near the docking point), or rent bikes for use in the area's nature trails. This is basically a rental establishment and "outfitter" store. ($/$$$)

DELLS WATER SPORTS / MIRROR LAKE RENTALS

3 Locations:

Highway 12 Bridge

Hiawatha Drive at Porta Vista

Mirror Lake State Park

☎   608-254-8702

⌗   dellswatersports.com

Dells Water Sports and Mirror Lake Rentals provides a comprehensive array of equipment and boat rentals for use on Lake Delton and Mirror Lake. They also serve as a full-service marina with a wide range of water-based activities, including parasailing, biking, hiking, skiing, fishing, and a lot more. With three locations throughout the Dells area, there is a lot of scenery and fun available.

Of particular note is the Mirror Lake Rentals facility. While Lake Delton offers much of the louder, engine-powered boating activity, Mirror Lake State Park is a quiet and peaceful retreat. Located within Mirror Lake State Park, Mirror Lake Rentals offer paddle boats, kayaks and canoes, quiet pontoon boats and paddleboats. Since the lake is within a state park, the lake is restricted in terms of boat speed ("No Wake"), and the atmosphere feels very quiet and secluded. Vessels may be available for rent on an hourly or daily basis. Fishing licenses and equipment may also be available. (Seasonal) ($/$$$)

BEAVER SPRINGS FISHING PARK

600 Trout Road

☎   608-254-2735

🖱 beaverspringsfun.com

Beaver Springs has a large collection of outdoor and nature-centric activities, making it a good stop for visitors wishing to experience some of the Dells more popular activities. The indoor and outdoor **Beaver Springs Public Aquarium** is open year-round and features over a thousand different species of fish in about 80,000 gallons of water. The **Beaver Springs Riding Stable** offers a one-hour long guided tour on

horseback that explores the Wisconsin Dells' wild side.

A major draw is the **Beaver Springs Fishing Park**. Here, visitors may choose from a wide variety of fishing options. Visitors may try for big game fish such as Bass and Walleye, or catch from any one of their 7 ponds for trout of various sizes and descriptions. Visitors can fish on a catch-and-release policy, or they can keep what they catch and even have it cooked up at nearby restaurants. No fishing permit is required. A great location for families who enjoy the outdoors, the facility is open year-round with limited wintertime attractions. ($/$$)

BOO CANOE & RAFT

S5127 Highway 113

☎   608-356-8856

🖱 boocanoe.com

In Baraboo, Boo Canoe & Raft allows visitors to rent various types of non-motorized boating equipment and cast off onto the Baraboo River. Several different trip choices are available, including tours of the Baraboo Rapids, scenic trips, and inflatable raft trips. Excursions can last as little as an hour and as long as 9 hours. Some excursions even allow visitors to travel on the river right past the Circus World Museum. Boo Canoe also offers launching capabilities for those who own their own boat. (Seasonal) ($/$$$)

STATE PARKS

Wisconsin loves nature! Outside of the Dells (but still nearby) are two major state parks: the Mirror Lake State Park and the Devil's Lake State Park. For a more genuine outdoor experience (and less tourist kitsch), consider making a trip to one of these places.

MIRROR LAKE STATE PARK
Route 23 off I-94
☎ 608-254-2333
🖱 mirrorlakewisconsin.com

Mirror Lake is a long, thin lake fed from the waters of Lake Delton. However, unlike the bustling Lake Delton, Mirror Lake rests in quiet seclusion, protected on all sides by the Mirror Lake State Park. Only three short miles from Wisconsin Dells, the park is the closest truly natural environment.

Surrounded by wilderness, the park offers many nature-based activities, including boating on the serene Mirror Lake. Visitors may rent canoes, kayaks, and other boats of minimal natural impact and take them out for short or long excursions on the lake. Also available are campsites,

hiking trails, and even a fishing pier. Certain activities may require a permit or additional payment. On the premises are also campsites and cabins, including one designed by Frank Lloyd Wright.

The park is open year-round, and the activities vary depending on the season. ($)

DEVIL'S LAKE STATE PARK
S5975 Park Road
☎ 608-356-8301
🖱 devilslakewisconsin.com

Located among 9,000 acres of pristine natural wilderness, Devil's Lake State Park is one of the most popular natural vacation destinations in all of Wisconsin. Over 1.1 million visitors make their way to this massive park to partake in all sorts of outdoor activities. It is located just south of Baraboo, less than 20 miles from Wisconsin Dells.

Devil's Lake itself is small; it is located near the visitor's center and much of the main activity. On the lake people may swim and boat. No gasoline motors are allowed, which keeps the lake quiet and relatively clean. There are beaches along the shore for swimming and relaxing. Winter recreation includes cross-country skiing, ice fishing and skating, and even snow-shoeing.

However, throughout the rest of the park are countless nature trails and activities. Standard activities such as biking, hiking, camping and fishing (permits may be required) are allowed here in designated places. Of primary interest (like much of the Dells area) are rock formations that were formed during glacial movements of the ice age. ($)

Area Attractions

Wisconsin Dells' attractions reach far beyond the tours and waterparks. There are so many ways to spend a dollar that visitors oftentimes are very surprised to see such a tourist Mecca in south-central Wisconsin. There are parks, museums, haunted houses, horse riding stables, and tons of shopping possibilities all along the strip of the Wisconsin Dells Parkway and through Downtown Dells.

Contents:
Museums
Walk-Through Attractions
Train Experiences
Live Shows
Fun for Grown-Ups
Golf Courses
Fudge and Sweets
Other Fun Things

There's a thin line between love and hate when it comes to wax museums, haunted houses, and other types of walk-through and interactive attractions. This section attempts to differentiate between these, when in fact there is often no need to; many follow similar structures of entertainment.

MUSEUMS

Wisconsin Dells is home to many different kinds of museums. But don't expect much dells-related-history or highbrow culture here. Instead, these museums are geared towards the odd, the amusing, the shocking, and the just plain fun. Some of these are wax museums, some have genuine artifacts, and some are a combination. In any case, their intent is to entertain as well as educate.

RIPLEY'S BELIEVE IT OR NOT! MUSEUM
115 Broadway
☎ 608-253-7556
🖮 ripleys.com

In a town already famous for its haunted houses and wax muse- ums, the quintessential Ripley's is still  the best. Located in the center of the Downtown Dells area, the building's façade is instantly recognizable as a kind of wacky, ancient archeological find. Inside, explore two floors of oddities, including King Tut's tomb, a car carved out of wood, and of course the classic Ripley exhibits. The museum features eight galleries, several video presentations and many eerie surprises.

Ever since Robert Ripley began showing off his findings at the first Odditorium in Chicago around the 1930s, the unusual and fascinating artifacts contained in his museums have mesmerized people. The chain of Ripley's museums spans the globe. Annually these museums receive about 12 million visitors. Among the other ventures of Ripley's Entertainment around America are aquariums, haunted houses, and miniature golf.

The Ripley's museum of Wisconsin Dells is open year-round. ($$)

H. H. BENNETT STUDIO AND HISTORY CENTER
215 Broadway
☎ 608-253-3523
Photographer Henry Hamilton Bennett is credited as being one of the pioneers of Dells-area tourism (the photograph of the leap at Stand Rock is perhaps his most famous). In 1875 he ac-

quired this studio to further explore his work. In particular, he took thousands of "Stereo Photographs," which when properly viewed through a stereoscope, would provide the illusion of a 3D landscape.

Bennett passed away in 1908, and his studio has been restored to its original condition as it was at that time. Today visitors can see much of Bennett's work and learn about the early history of Wisconsin tourism. Among the displays are some of his original photographic equipment, Native American products (sold to tourists of the day), and Bennett's daughter's doll exhibit. The museum is open most of the year, with limited off-season hours. ($$)

CIRCUS WORLD MUSEUM
550 Water Street
☎ 608-356-8341
⌂ circusworldmuseum.com
The town of Baraboo may not be a house-hold name. But it was here, in 1884, where brothers John, Charles, Alf T., Otto, and Al Ringling founded the Ringling Bros. Circus. Wisconsin would become well-known for "winter-

ing" circus troupes, as more than 100 traveling companies would eventually park themselves in this area during the off-show months. However, it was the Ringling Bros. Circus that put Baraboo on the map of circus-dom.

John. M. Kelley, who worked closely with the Ringling Bros. Circus as their lawyer, created the Circus World Museum in 1954 as a way to preserve the fast-declining circus show. The museum is located on the original site of the Ringling Bros. winter quarters. Today, the museum immortalizes the bygone era of railroad traveling circus shows. Over 100,000 people visit the attraction each year.

The museum has been a highlight for children and families of all ages for years. This headlining year-round attraction is both indoors and outdoors, and features all kinds of circus-related memorabilia and exhibits, such as an impressive collection of 200

restored and preserved circus wagons. They have seasonal events, such as an annual summertime circus parade. In many ways, being at Circus World is like being at a traveling circus. ($)

MUSEUM OF HISTORIC TORTURE DEVICES
740 Eddy Street
☎   608-254-2439
Warning: this attraction may not me suitable for families.

This museum fulfills its promise to deliver a lot of gory and startling images and unthinkable devices of pain, but it seems really out of place in a predominantly family-oriented vacation destination. Among the items on display are the Cucking Stool, Death Cage, and The Rack. Most of the pain involves poking or stretching – see how cruel mankind is to each other in this off-color attraction.

WALK-THROUGH ATTRACTIONS ——————————

If you want to be intrigued by movie-like sets, explore dark and dreary dungeons, or even get scared a bit, consider a visit to one of the Dells' area walk-through attractions. At these places, visitors generally follow a one-way path through an indoor environment designed to give a particular experience – be it fun, scary, or somewhere in between. These aren't wax museums; visitors won't learn very much of real value, but they can be quite fun.

TOMMY BARTLETT'S EXPLORATORY

560 Wisconsin Dells Parkway
☎   608-254-2525
🖰   tommybartlett.com

Tommy Bartlett opened "Tommy Bartlett's Robot World & Exploratory" in 1982. Situated next to his ever-popular thrill show, the futuristic satellite-ship-shaped building attracted thousands of visitors. The attraction kept its popularity with a robot-guided tour of a "house of the future", but as time passed it began to show its age. Today, the Tommy Bartlett Exploratory has largely dropped the robot motif, and evolved from a rather science fiction look at technology and the future to a full-blown interactive science museum.

Children and families will particularly enjoy the exhibits, which include exhibits on electricity (including a popular Van de Graff electricity exhibit to "make your hair stand on end"), a spinning, ride-able gyro, a unique bicycle-on-a-high-wire experience, and dozens of others, large and small, which help kids and adults

alike learn about the scientific world around them.

Headlining the Exploratory is an original Russian **MIR Space Station** (the only one currently on display out of three in existence). The station is the core module, and stretches about 43 feet long. Visitors can explore this station – both inside and out – and learn about some unique aspects of space travel.

Overall, the Tommy Bartlett Exploratory, open year-round, is a popular highlight for many families visiting the Dells, and for kids, it is well worth the visit. ($$)

TOP SECRET

527 Wisconsin Dells Parkway
☎   608-254-6700
🖰   dellstopsecret.com

It is easy to recognize: Top Secret is the only building on the Wisconsin Dells Parkway designed to look like an upside-down White House. This walk-through attraction takes visitors on a guided tour of this White House. Marketing efforts for this attraction give little indication as to the contents, and this curiosity is certainly part of the draw. The attraction is not very scary (it is not a haunted house). It starts out when visitors are led into several famous rooms of the White House (turned upside-down, of course), and then we learn what happened. ($/$$)

THE WONDER SPOT
100 Scott Drive
☎ 608-254-4224
At The Wonder Spot, water flows upwards, people shrink and stretch, balls roll against gravity, and chairs balance at odd angles. Of course, these are all based on one popular optical illusion, which is immediately apparent upon entering the attraction: the room is slanted sideways. However, even knowing the secret does not deter your eyes from being tricked – so the attraction still works. The Wonder Spot makes for an enjoyable diversion; it is kind of like a playground of cool special effects. ($)

WIZARD QUEST
105 Broadway
☎ 608-254-2184
⌨ wizardquest.net
A very unusual and new kind of interactive attraction, Wizard Quest is a combination of an in-

teractive video game and a walk-through fun house, complete with schoolyard-style slides. Designed with a medieval fairy tale setting in mind (dragons and such), it is basically a playground with a purpose. When you enter, you are told that you have a specific mission, and to accomplish this mission you must solve all kinds of puzzles. Visitors (adults and children) explore the different "realms" as they attempt solve puzzles and accomplish the mission. There is a time limit for visitors who take too long to complete a quest.

The attraction has the air of a haunted house – which is a deterrent for the younger sect. However, once beyond the introduction, it is not really very scary (with few exceptions) and a heck of a lot of fun. ($$)

ALIEN PLANET
228 Broadway
☎ 608-253-5055
⌨ alienplanet.us
Aliens have landed in the Dells! This unique haunted house-type walk-through attraction is a mix of 3D screens, wax figures, and various sets. At the start, visitors don 3D goggles and walk through a secret scientific lab-type facility

where aliens and other various creatures are being experimented on. As the "story" goes, some of the aliens escape, and scare visitors as they journey along.

DUNGEON OF HORRORS
819 Elm Street
☎   608-254-2980
🖑   timefantasy.com
When it first opened in 1981, Dungeon of Horrors was initially meant to be a historical re-creation of a medieval dungeon, providing visitors with an educational look at the past. Since then, however, it has evolved into an all-out haunted house as visitors traverse the dungeon, getting spooked every which way. The attraction uses live actors to scare visitors, and it may not be suitable for the faint of heart or young children. ($)

GHOST OUT-POST
633 Wisconsin Dells Parkway
☎   608-254-2127
The Ghost Out-Post haunted house features many frightening scenes, including several animatronic characters designed to scare all who enter. The attraction has been recently updated to include additional scenes. This attraction features dark room, maze-like

ambience, and is not recommended for the faint of heart. ($)

LOONY BIN
633 Wisconsin Dells Parkway
☎   608-254-2127
The Loony Bin is a fun house. It's not very scary, and its more suited for people who would prefer to skip out on the haunted houses of the area, but who still want to enjoy a walk-through attraction. It features standard illusions and various "fun" effects and things to see and do. ($)

HAUNTED MANSION
112 Broadway
☎   608-254-7513
While still providing its share of fright, the Haunted Mansion is one of the less scary haunted house attractions within Wisconsin Dells. The scenes are primarily animatronic characters, creepy noises, strobe lights, and other effects. Though its still scary, if you want to brave a haunted house without it being too intense, the Haunted Mansion is a good choice – it's more of a special effects house than a fright house (though it has its share of fright as well – so enter with caution). ($)

DELLS MINING CO.

427 Broadway &
1480 Wisconsin Dells Parkway
☎   608-253-7002
🖰   dellsminingco.com

What back-breaking labor used to put food on the table for hundreds of years is now available as a tourist attraction! At the Dells Mining Co., people (particularly children and their families), are given the opportunity to pan for gold from collections of soil collected from gem-rich fields in North Carolina.

Participants purchase boxes of the soil and pan for valuable contained therein – using traditional equipment. All sorts of naturally-occurring valuables may be found in the soil, and visitors can keep everything they find!

The Broadway location is open year-round, and the Parkway location is open seasonally. ($$)

LASER STORM OF WISCONSIN DELLS

501 Broadway
☎   608-254-4855
🖰   laser-storm.com

Laser tag is just as the name sounds – a game of schoolyard "tag" with futuristic light guns instead of hands. At Laser Storm, players (split into 2 teams) are equipped with the standard laser tag apparatus, including gun and light sensor. Then, after instruction, they are released into the combat zone.

The Laser Storm arena is a dark, futuristic indoor "battlefield" lit with black light and filled with plenty of objects to hide behind. The goal of this game is to shoot the opposing team (with the provided light gun) as many times as possible. Players' equipment senses when he/she has been tagged. A full game lasts 12 minutes.

Laser Storm is best suited for larger groups of friends, though it is possible to play in smaller groups or even join an existing group.

TRAIN EXPERIENCES

Museums, rides, historical preservation, and the Wisconsin Dells countryside all make for an area ripe for train-related attraction. The train hub of America – Chicago – is a short 200 miles away, so these unique pieces of American transportation history fit well within the Dells.

MID-CONTINENT RAILWAY MUSEUM

E8948 Diamond Hill Road
☎ 608-522-4261
🖰 midcontinent.org

Railroad history junkies, take note: you'll be hard-pressed to find a more comprehensive, more complete collection of authentic railroad cars from 1885-1915 (the "Golden Age" of rail transit) anywhere else in the world. At the Mid-Continent Railway Museum in North Freedom (near Baraboo), over 100 pieces of authentic, restored equipment are on display, including steam engines, passenger and freight cars, cabooses, and miscellaneous railroad equipment. Each piece is documented with its origin and restoration process.

The highlight of this museum is a 50-minute, 7-mile ride on an authentic train, built from restored passenger cars of 1915. Passengers board from an original 1894 train depot, the train atten-
dants wear authentic uniforms, and the train takes visitors through the scenic Baraboo countryside. The journey feels particularly designed for children, but any train-nut will enjoy the historic trip. (Seasonal, but with special off-season rides) ($$)

BLACK BART'S OLD #9

420 State Road 13
☎ 608-253-2278.
🖰 blackbartsbuffet.com

This is a very uniquely-conceived attraction that can also be lots of fun for families as an old-west-centered environment. It is Black Bart's Buffet, which features barbeque, roast beef, potatoes, and other classic dishes. It is Black Bart's Shooting Range, with animatronics for targets. It is also a video arcade, with arcade and redemption games.

Most importantly, it is Black Bart's Old #9, a short train ride around the property. Mostly geared for younger train enthusiasts, it is a miniature train complete with operator. It's a nice, family-friendly experience. ($/$$)

RIVERSIDE & GREAT NORTHERN RAILROAD

N115 County Road N
☎ 608-254-6367
🖱 randgn.com

As an entry into the Dells train experiences, the Riverside & Great Northern Railroad operates a 15" gauge railroad that takes visitors on a 3 mile round trip tour of the countryside. The trip lasts about 30 minutes. It is a simple and pleasant getaway from the nearby bustling downtown area. The attraction also features a railroad museum and café for some lounging before and after a trip.

The railway began its history in the 1940s in Janesville, Wisconsin, as a way of advertising steam engines. The attraction moved into Wisconsin Dells about a decade later, where they continued to operate until the organization went bankrupt in 1980. About 8 years later, it was turned into a non-for-profit attraction, and eventually reopened. Today it operates regularly touring the tourist season. (Seasonal) ($/$$)

LIVE SHOWS

Magic, circus fun, country music, dinner shows… if it's live entertainment you seek, the Dells seeks to fulfill.

TOMMY BARTLETT THRILL SHOW

560 Wisconsin Dells Parkway
☎ 608-254-2525
🖱 tommybartlett.com

Well, this is it – the original skiing thrill show, and the major reason why Wisconsin Dells is on the map as the prime tourist destination it is today. For over 50 years, the Tommy Bartlett Thrill Show has been the main tourist attraction at Wisconsin Dells for thousands of people and families. And even today, after such a long and illustrious run, the show is still as great as ever. Tommy Bartlett may not be a household name for those who live outside the Midwest, but to the millions in the area, he has defined the aquatic thrill show, bringing people back to the Dells year after year.

When it began its run in 1952, it was a traveling show, and Wisconsin Dells was the second stop on the tour. It traveled to many national (and some international) locations. The show expanded as the years progressed, and eventually found itself as a permanent fixture on the Wisconsin Dells Parkway.

The show today is an absolute hoot, with daily summertime performances on the waters of Lake Delton. Visitors are seated in an outdoor grandstand-like theater facing the lake as they watch breathtaking balancing acts on water skis (such as the famous water ski pyramid), speed boats jumping off ramps and out of the water, amazing jumps, dives, and (on special nights and times) hang-gliding, fireworks and light shows. The show is so diverse that it even includes clown acts, juggling, comedy routines, acrobatics, and motorcycle stunts. This is one not-to-be-missed event. ($$)

WISCONSIN OPRY
E10964 Moon Road
☎ 608-254-7951
🖰 wisconsinopry.com
If you like American country cooking and country music, you may want to check out the Wisconsin Opry in nearby Baraboo. This lively show features classic country food, and live entertainment featuring songs performed by resident musicians. The show has regular performances during the summer tourist season. (Seasonal) ($$)

RICK WILCOX THEATER
1666 Wisconsin Dells Parkway
☎ 608-254-5511
🖰 rickwilcox.com
Until recently, the best place to see top-of-the-line stage magic shows was in Las Vegas. However, the popularity of Las Vegas-type magic shows has grown immensely in the past several years, and other tourist towns are opening resident magic shows of their own.

Magician Rick Wilcox has had a touring magic show for over 15 years, during which he has become known as master of sleight-of-hand. In 1999, he (along with his wife, Susan) opened a theater in Wisconsin

Dells devoted exclusively to his magic show. Since then, the duo has dazzled audiences with all the classic illusions of stage magic, including invisibility and levitation effects, and many other well-known routines.

The Rick Wilcox Theater seats about 600 people. The magic show runs year-round and lasts about 90 minutes. ($$/$$$)

CRYSTAL GRAND MUSIC THEATRE
430 Munroe Street
☎ 608-254-4545
⌂ crystalgrand.com
With seating for 2000 in a secluded 22-acre environment, the Crystal Grand Music Theatre is a performance venue. It features a regular rotation of touring performers. Though musical performances fill up most of the schedule, other acts – such as comics – make appearances at Crystal Grand. Information about purchasing tickets may be obtained directly from the box office. ($$$)

FAB '50S LIVE
4031 River Road
☎ 608-254-4810
⌂ fab50slive.com
Located at the Chula Vista Resort, the Fab '50s Live is a musical tribute to the decade that popularized Rock 'n Roll. Complete with live musicians, dancers, and well-known songs of the decade, the show is interactive for the whole family. Famous singers/songwriters are impersonated – such as Jerry Lee Lewis, Buddy Holly, and the king himself, Elvis.

There are matinee and evening performances, and even a buffet-style dinner is available. The show plays primarily during the tourist season but they may have special holiday shows during the wintertime. Ticket information may be obtained by visiting the website or by calling their phone number. ($$$)

THUNDER VALLEY INN DINNER SHOW
W15344 Waubeek Road
☎ 608-254-4145
⌂ thundervalleyinn.com
The Thunder Valley Inn, a traditional Scandinavian farm that boasts genuine hospitality, has been in the Dells area for over 130 years. It is home to a bed &

breakfast, farm tours, a restaurant, and the Thunder Valley Inn Show.

There are several shows throughout the day, which feature traditional Scandinavian songs and instruments (fiddle and accordion), comedy and storytelling. The show has a very quaint and intimate feeling, and is billed as being absolutely family-friendly. The dinner served may include such homestyle dishes as pot roast and garden vegetables, salad, and dessert. ($$)

AL RINGLING THEATRE
136 4th Avenue
☎ 608-356-8864
✎ alringling.com
Just after the turn of the 20th century, Baraboo native Al Ringling was an extremely powerful man. He was famous for his circus, and would travel the world. As what some consider a his "gift

to the city," he created the Al Ringling Theatre which was reminiscent of the opera houses he fell in love with as he traveled through many European countries. The theatre began construction in March of 1915, and was opened for business a mere seven months later.

The interior of the theatre has the classic opera look; a circular auditorium with a stage on the far end, and intricately ornate on both. At its tallest, it is about 70 feet high. It currently seats over 800 people, and has 17 boxes lining the perimeter. Visitors can get tours of this historic theater in Baraboo. The theatre also has concert performances, plays, movies, and various special events. Information about the performance schedule is available by calling or visiting their web site. ($)

FUN FOR GROWN-UPS

I was originally going to call this section "Adult Entertainment" but that carries with it a certain weight that I didn't want associated with this family-friendly destination. The attractions here are for the big kids – spending the day at Wisconsin Dells does not mean having to truck through waterparks and wax museums without a chaperone. True, it's primarily a family place, and the Dells atmosphere encourages adults to unleash the child within, but following are attractions designed for the grown-ups.

HO-CHUNK CASINO
S3214 U.S. Highway 12
☎ 608-356-6210
🖰 ho-chunk.com

The Ho-Chunk Nation of Indians inhabited the Wisconsin Dells (and much of Wisconsin in general) for many hundreds of years. Today the nation operates several casino areas throughout Wisconsin, including Majestic Pines and Rainbow Casino. In Baraboo (near the Dells) is their largest and best resort, the Ho-Chunk Casino Hotel & Convention Center.

The resort is an easy drive from the Dells tourist area (many hotels have shuttle services available). The casino floor features over 2,400 slot machines, over forty blackjack tables, and a large, complete Bingo parlor. The slot machines are available 24 hours a day, and Bingo is offered specific times throughout the day. Table games run on varying schedules. Regular players at any of Ho-Chunk facilities throughout Wisconsin might want to consider joining their player's club, which credits the amount of play.

The resort has accommodations available on-site; everything from standard rooms to full luxury suites with all kinds of amenities. There are several restaurants too, ranging from fine dining to a quick-bite café. Also on the property is an entertainment venue that features topical traveling talent such as comedy and music shows. Tickets for events may be purchased at the Guest Services Center. Most attractions, including shows, require the attendee to be 21 years old or over, the gambling age of Ho-Chunk. Fitness equipment and a swimming pool (with kiddie pool) is also available on-property for an additional daily use fee.

Notwithstanding this grown-up playground, the Dells is a family vacation destination. As such, Ho-Chunk is home to Kids Quest, the largest hourly child care provider in the United States. The facility is basically a large indoor playground for the young ones. It has climbing facilities, computer games, karaoke, and television. Kids Quest is strictly for very young kids, which leaves an unfortunate gap in entertainment options for older children and teens that aren't yet able to gamble. ($/$$$$)

WOLLERSHEIM WINERY
7876 Highway 188
☎   608-643-6515
🖰 wollersheim.com

Wisconsin is a cheese state, not a wine state like California or New York, but that doesn't preclude the presence of this first-class winery. About 30 miles south of the Wisconsin Dells, in Prairie du Sac, is the Wollersheim Winery. Overlooking a slope on the Wisconsin River, the winery offers tours, some tasting, and purchasing of their various kinds of wine. The tours are regularly scheduled, and last about an hour. All ages can participate in the tour, but only visitors ages 21 and over can participate in the wine tasting.

Although the current state of the winery dates to 1972, the history goes back to the 1840s. However, some disappointing sales caused the owner, Count Agoston Haraszthy of Hungary, to move his business to California, and later became famous for the wines he produced there. During the Civil War period, Peter Kehl took over the property and built the buildings that are there today – they are listed on the National Register of Historic Places. They produce about 165,000 gallons of wine each year. ($)

SALOONS OF THE DOWNTOWN DELLS

A stroll through the Downtown Dells (which is the "official" City of Wisconsin Dells) is a great way for grown-ups to spend time away from the family hustle of the Parkway. In this stretch of town a little more than a mile long rests many gift shops, restaurants, bars, gift shops, candy stores, and even more gift shops. It's a great place to mosey around without a lot of planning ahead. Some parts of the stretch are loud, and some parts are quiet, but even at night there is activity in the area. Of course, most of these bars and saloons have restaurants that happily cater to families as well.

Some of the offerings are: **Mama's Night Club** (731 Eddy Street, 608-254-6262), with music and dancing, **Country Keg Saloon** (713 Oak Street, 608-254-7475), with family food service, and **Showboat Saloon** (24 Broadway, 608-253-2628).

GOLF COURSES

Wisconsin Dells is no stranger to golfing; though miniature golf is prominent along the strip and in several resorts, the area is home to several full-size courses with various difficulty ratings. Most golf courses in the area are open seasonally, though some may have winter use for their grounds (such as snowmobile or ski trails). Following is a select list of full-size area public golf courses.

CHRISTMAS MOUNTAIN VILLAGE GOLF
S944 Christmas Mountain Road
☎ 608-254-3971
🖰 christmasmountainvillage.com
The multi-purpose Christmas Mountain Village resort is home to two golf courses, the **Oaks Golf Course** and the **Pines Golf Course**. The Oaks Course consists of a full 18-holes, and the Pines Course is a shorter nine. Golf lessons are also available. In the wintertime, the course becomes a cross-country ski paradise (see elsewhere in this book for resort information).

COLDWATER CANYON GOLF COURSE
4052 River Road
☎ 608-254-8489
🖰 wisconsindellsgolf.com

Adjacent to the Chula Vista Resort, Coldwater Canyon is 18 holes of regulation golf, plus a practice driving range. The two sections of the course (9 holes each) were built over 70 years apart, and golfers may decide to golf on the full 18, or they may decide to play a smaller portion.

PINECREST GOLF COURSE
712 State Road 23
☎ 608-254-2165
🖰 dellspar3golf.com
Pinecrest is a Par 3 Course – a bit easier and more suitable to amateur or fair-weather golfers not looking to absorb a full day on their golf outing. They bill themselves as being a particularly family-friendly course (which is ideal for the Dells).

WILDERNESS WOODS GOLF CLUB
856 Canyon Road
☎ 608-253-4653
🖱 golfwildernesswoods.com
Part of the massive Wilderness Resort complex, the Wilderness Woods Golf Club is a full 18-hole course. On the property are also the **Whispering Pines Restaurant** and a pro shop. One of the most distinctive features of Wilderness Woods is the **Little Links** course. This is an actual golf course – not mini-golf – scaled down in size for younger golfers. It is six holes of easy golfing, wide fairways, and friendly hazards.

TRAPPERS TURN GOLF CLUB
652 Trappers Turn Drive
☎ 608-253-7000
🖱 trappersturn.com

The Trappers Turn Golf Club features 27 holes divided into three sections; golfers may play either 9 or 18 holes. Nine hole plays may not always be available, depending on how crowded the course is.

SPRING BROOK GOLF RESORT
175 Berry Lane
☎ 608-254-4343
🖱 dellsgolfresort.com
Spring Brook is a private golf community that has allowed public access to its par 3, 9-hole golf course. The course is surrounded by private homes and vacation rental properties, and although the public is welcome, the course is largely for residents.

FUDGE AND SWEETS

If the waterparks and walk-through attractions don't leave their mark on a traveler, then the sheer amount of candy and fudge shops in the Dells, particularly in the downtown area, definitely will. Following is a select list of fun impulse sweet shops, but don't necessarily use this list as a must-see guide – just by walking through the downtown Dells you will pass many, many of these stores.

SWISS MAID FUDGE

743 Superior Street

☎ 608-254-7771

✍ dellsfudge.com

This shop opened in 1962, and sells all kinds of fudge varieties, taffy, chocolate and other sweets. Many of the goods are made on the premises.

ORIGINAL WISCONSIN DELLS FUDGE

108 Broadway

☎ 608-253-3373

Original Wisconsin Dells Fudge makes and sells many kinds of candy, fudge, and other homemade treats.

KERNEL POPCORN'S FACTORY

460 Broadway

☎ 608-254-6880

Located in the Bavarian Village complex in the downtown Dells area, this shop sells many, many (some sources claim 25) different flavors of popcorn.

CANDY CORNER

400 Broadway

☎ 608-253-4000

Also located in the Bavarian Village in downtown Dells is Candy Corner, which sells various kinds of sweets, as well as coffee and ice cream.

GRANDMA'S ORIGINAL FUDGE

26 Broadway

☎ 608-254-6443

This shop sells chocolate and fudge creations, candy corn, jellybeans, and various other sweets.

GOODY GOODY GUM DROP

401 Broadway

☎ 608-253-7983

✍ goodygumdrop.com

This store boasts itself as the largest candy store in Wisconsin Dells. All kinds of candy, chocolate, taffy, fudge, gummy candies, and so much more are for sale here. The store has 2 locations; the one downtown (phone number listed above) and one within Riverview Park. The downtown location is open year-round.

OTHER FUN THINGS ——————————

The diversity of the Dells demands this section, which lists attractions that don't fit into another category. From movies to mini-golf, there is so much to do in the Dells.

PIRATE'S COVE ADVENTURE GOLF
Highways 12/13/16 & 23
☎ 608-254-7500
🖑 piratescovewisdells.com

Pirate's Cove Adventure Golf is already one the largest (if not *the* largest) chain of miniature golf courses. And Wisconsin Dells is home to the largest one in the entire United States. This place is huge, and it draws equally huge crowds. Pirate's Cove is an extremely family-oriented place; expect lots of children golfing.

The course contains five – yes, *five* – full-featured 18-hole miniature golf courses for visitors to play. On and around the course are thousands and thousands of plants, 17 waterfalls, countless rivers and rock formations, and certain holes even provide a view of the Wisconsin River. There is little shade across the landscape (though there are some trees and a few other shady holes), but its late operating hours and bright night lights allow it to stay open during the cooler hours of the hottest days.

Pirate's Cove Adventure Golf began on the small lakeside town of Traverse City, Michigan, in 1983. Today they have over 20 locations nationwide, including Orlando, Bar Harbor, Branson, Lake George, Lake Placid, and Williamsburg, Virginia. They have won many awards for being the "best mini-golf course" in several states.

In addition to golfing, the Wisconsin Dells facility also has a small video arcade on the premises. For younger children, there is also a small "playland" – a playground with slides, a suspension bridge, and other jungle-gym-type diversions. ($/$$)

BIG SKY TWIN DRIVE-IN THEATRE
Highway 16 East
☎ 608-254-8025
🖑 bigskydrivein.com

The days of drive-in movies are alive and well at Wisconsin Dells!

The Big Sky Twin Drive-In Theatre is a throwback to the days of watching double features in your car! Big Sky's two screens give visitors a choice of 2 double features, all of which are brand new first-run movies.

How it works: visitors drive up in their car, choose a parking space facing a huge outdoor screen, and sit back and relax while they watch two movies in a row! More than anything else, it's a chance to see two movies for the price of one in a very special way. There are two separate screens, each with one show nightly beginning around twilight. The theater is only open during the summer tourist season. ($/$$)

PAINT IT! POTTERY SHOP
332 Highway 13
☎   608-254-5466
🖱 paintitpotteryshop.com
Painting ready-made pottery is a popular and well-established way to express artistic talents for peo-

ple of all ages. At Paint It! Pottery Shop, visitors choose from about 400 different kinds of pottery and a plethora of paint. For a daily use fee plus cost of items to be decorated, anybody can sit around all day and create masterpiece after masterpiece. This is a very well-conceived and thoroughly-equipped establishment. ($$)

OLD RIVER & TOTEM POLE MINI-GOLF
Eddy Street (Downtown Dells)
☎   608-254-8336
Old River in Downtown Dells is a small miniature golf course. It features up to 27 holes (visitors can play shorter games if they wish). The major advantage to this course is its close proximity to shopping and other downtown attractions. ($/$$)

DETOUR: POLITICS OF PECK

George Wilbur Peck served as governor of Wisconsin from 1891 to 1895. However, he is best known a newspaper humorist and creator of several on-going sketches (including his most famous "Peck's Bad Boy"). He even created his own comedy newspaper. Many of his stories and articles had political slants. As compiled in Beck's Compendium of Fun, following is a short story which takes place near Kilbourn City (now Wisconsin Dells). Without the heavy development of tourism, the Dells was a vacation destination with little more than the rocks themselves, a place for those with means to gather. It is a chance to better understand what the Dells meant to those around the turn of the 20th century.

WOMAN-DOZING A DEMOCRAT

A fearful tale conies to us from Columbus. A party of prominent citizens of that place took a trip to the Dells of Wisconsin one day last week. It was composed of ladies and gentlemen of both political parties, and it was hoped that nothing would occur to mar the pleasure of the excursion.

When the party visited the Dells, Mr. Chapin, a lawyer of Democratic proclivities, went out upon a rock overhanging a precipice, or words to that effect, and he became so absorbed in the beauty of the scene that he did not notice a Republican lady who left the throng and waltzed softly up behind him. She had blood in her eye and gum in her mouth, and she grasped the lawyer, who is a weak man, by the arms, and hissed in his ear

"Hurrah for Garfield, or I will plunge you headlong into the yawning gulf below!"

It was a trying moment. Chapin rather enjoyed being held by a woman, but not in such a position that, if she let go her hold to spit on her hands, he would go a hundred feet down, and become as flat as the Greenback party, and have to be carried home in a basket.

In a sec ond he thought over all the sins of his past life, which was pretty quick work, as anybody will admit who knows the man. He thought of how he would be looked down upon by Gabe Bouck, and all the fellows, if it once got out that he had been frightened into going back on his party.

He made up his mind that he would die before he would hurrah for Garfield, but when the merciless woman pushed him towards the edge of the rock, and, "Last call! Yell, or down you go!" he opened his mouth and yelled so they heard it in Kilbourn City:

"Hurrah for Garfield! Now lemme go!"

Though endowed with more than ordinary eloquence, no remarks that he had ever made before brought the applause that this did. Everybody yelled, and the woman smiled as pleasantly as though she had not crushed the young life out of her victim, and left him a bleeding sacrifice on the altar of his country, but when she had realized what she had done her heart smote her, and she felt bad.

Chapin will never be himself again. From that moment his proud spirit was broken, and all during the picnic he seemed to have lost his cud. He leaned listlessly against a tree, pale as death, and fanned himself with a skimmer. When the party had spread the lunch on the ground and gathered around, sitting on the ant-hills, he sat down with them mechanically, but his appetite was gone, and when that is gone there is not enough of him left for a quorum.

Friends rallied around him, passed the pickles, and drove the ant-mires out of a sandwich, and handed it to him on a piece of shingle, but he either passed or turned it down. He said he couldn't take a trick. Later on, when the lemonade was brought on, the flies were skimmed off of some of it, and a little colored water was put in to make it look inviting, but his eyes were sot. He said they couldn't fool him. After what had occurred, he didn't feel as though any Democrat was safe. He expected to be poisoned on account of his politics, and all he asked was to live to get home.

Nothing was left undone to rally him, and cause him to forget the fearful scene through which he had passed. Only once did he partially come to himself, and show an interest in worldly affairs, and that was when it was found that he had sat down on some raspberry jam with his white pants on. When told of it, he smiled a ghastly smile, and said they were all welcome to his share of the jam.

They tried to interest him in conversation by drawing war maps with three-tined folks on the jam, but he never showed that he knew what they were about until Mr. Moak, of Watertown, took a brush, made of cauliflower preserved in mustard, and shaded the lines of the war map on Mr. Chapin's trousers, which Mr. Butterfield had drawn in the jam. Then his artistic eye took in the incongruity of the colors, and he gasped for breath, and said:

"Moak, that is played out. People will notice it."

But he relapsed again into semi-unconsciousness, and never spoke again, not a great deal, till he got home.

He has ordered that there be no more borrowing of sugar and drawings of tea back and forth between his house and that of the lady who broke his heart, and be has announced that he will go without saurkraut all winter rather than borrow a machine for cutting cabbage of a woman that would destroy the political prospects of a man who had never done a wrong in his life.

He has written to the chairman of the Democratic State Central Committee to suspend judgment on his case, until he can explain how it happened that a dyed-in-the-wood Democrat hurrahed for Garfield.

Stand Rock of today… not quite H. H. Bennett

Baranger Motions at Ripley's *Believe It or Not!* Museum in Orlando

Gardens at House on the Rock

Yours Truly in Downtown Dells

Eating and Sleeping

While far from exhaustive, this section gets the tourist a bit oriented as to what accommodations and restaurants are available within the Dells area.

SELECT RESTAURANTS

Wisconsin Dells is peppered with restaurants along the Parkway, with a high concentration in the Downtown area. Following is a list of select restaurants divided into these two sections. Chain restaurants (you know who they are) have been omitted here – but rest assured you'll be able to find that fast-food hamburger or milk-shake, should your seasoned stomach require it.

Price Overview:
$ - inexpensive (entrée: less than $15)
$$ - moderate (entrée: $15-$30)
$$$ - expensive (entrée: over $30)

AREA RESTAURANTS

Generally located along the Wisconsin Dells Parkway, these restaurants are noted for their specialties. These are not well-known chains (there are dozens of those in the Dells). These are special places, and unique dining experiences.

The Del-Bar
800 Wisconsin Dells Parkway
☎   608-253-1861
🖰   del-bar.com
Located on the Wisconsin Dells Parkway and one of the Dells' few truly upscale restaurant, the Del-Bar (located exactly between the Dells and Lake Delton), opened in the 1930s and was architectur-ally influenced by Frank Lloyd Wright. Today it serves varieties of steak, fish, and wine. ($$/$$$)

Ishnala Restaurant
S2011 Ishnala Road
☎   608-253-1771
🖰   ishnala.com
Located within the Mirror Lake State Park section of the Wiscon-

sin Dells area, Ishnala (meaning "alone") is one of the most beautiful restaurants in the area. It opened in 1953 with an intimate interior décor of an old Northwoods lodge, with heavy Native American influences. The restaurant overlooks Mirror Lake. Steak and lobster are on top of the list of food choices. Though it a casual establishment, there is an upscale ambience and high quality food. ($$/$$$)

Mr. Pancake Restaurant
1405 Wisconsin Dells Parkway
☎   608-253-3663
🖰   mrpancake.com
An unmistakable landmark building along the Parkway, Mr. Pancake is shaped like an old riv-

erboat. It has been around since the early 1960s and is a very laid-back family establishment. In addition to pancakes, they also have blintzes, hamburgers, salads, and other sandwiches. ($/$$)

Henny Penny
1010 Wisconsin Dells Parkway
☎   608-254-8093
This restaurant features casual family dining on the Wisconsin Dells Parkway. ($/$$)

BJ's Restaurant
1201 Wisconsin Dells Parkway
☎   608-254-6278
This restaurant features casual family dining on the Wisconsin Dells Parkway. ($/$$)

DOWNTOWN RESTAURANTS & BARS

The Downtown Dells is packed with restaurants: some known chains, some lesser-known chains, and some unique Wisconsin treats. Following is a select list of the latter. These are smaller and generally more intimate establishments than the restaurants located on the Parkway, with more of a rowdy, party atmosphere (though still generally family-friendly).

Essen Haus German Restaurant
414 Broadway
☎   608-253-7766
🖰   essen-haus.com

Part of the Bavarian Village, the Essen Haus features German food, live music, and is generally known as one of the better restaurants in Wisconsin Dells. ($$)

Famous Dave's Bar-B-Que
435 Broadway
☎ 608-253-6683
🖰 ribkingsofamerica.com
Restaurant is part of a nationwide chain, which features all kinds of ribs and rib-related dishes. ($/$$)

Paul Bunyan's Restaurant
411 Highway 13
☎ 608-254-8717
🖰 paulbunyans.com
One of several locations (another being in Minocqua), this restaurant is located west of Downtown Dells and features lumberjack food – pancakes, potatoes, fish, chicken, etc. ($/$$)

ACCOMMODATIONS

Wisconsin Dells' waterpark resorts are the major draw to the area, but the area is chock-full of all kinds of accommodations, mostly motel-style. In fact, area promotional material states that the Dells has more than 8,000 rooms and campsites. Following is a select list of area accommodations that do not necessarily have a waterpark on the premises (though they may have a pool or other such aquatic diversion).

Of course, there are many more hotels within the Dells area than are listed within this book; the ones here represent only a varied sampling. For a more thorough listing, utilize various travel agent services as Travelocity (travelocity.com) or Hotels.com (hotels.com). For price information, please contact the hotel directly.

Important: when selecting a hotel, please keep in mind that many hotels in Wisconsin Dells (particularly the smaller ones) are *seasonal*: they open in the spring and close in the fall.

WISCONSIN DELLS PARKWAY

These hotels are on the main Wisconsin Dells Parkway strip; many of them are smaller hotels, and some are larger. They are spread out along the approximately 3-mile strip.

Note: Even within the scope of this book, this list is *not* all-encompassing for accommodations within Wisconsin Dells. Specifically, it does not highlight the waterpark resorts. For a list of select hotels and resorts with extensive water-related activities, please see the appropriate section elsewhere in this book.

Econo Lodge Wisconsin Dells
350 West Munroe Street
☎ 608-253-4343
✆ dells-inn.com
This small motel is located just off the main strip, and has an indoor swimming pool.

Lakeside Motel
210 Wisconsin Dells Parkway
☎ 608-253-2282
✆ dells-lakeside.com
Located near the tip of Lake Delton, the motel has dock access and offers use of paddleboats and rowboats. Also features an outdoor pool and small video arcade.

American World Hotel Resort
400 Wisconsin Dells Parkway
☎ 608-253-4451
✆ americanworld.com
Hotel and recreation vehicle (R.V.) resort is located on a large 11-acre site, with indoor and outdoor pools (with small waterslides), tennis/volleyball courts, game room and food service.

Hilton Garden Inn Wisconsin Dells
101 East Hiawatha Drive
☎ 608-251-1100
✆ gardeninn.com
Just off the main strip, this full-featured large hotel (over 120 rooms) has fitness and pool facilities, gift shop, and more.

Mayflower Motel & Suites
910 Wisconsin Dells Parkway
☎ 608-253-6471
✆ dellsmayflower.com
This motel features indoor and outdoor pool, game room, picnic area, and lots of different levels of suites.

Alakai Hotel & Suites
1030 Wisconsin Dells Parkway
☎ 608-253-3803
✆ alakaihotel.com
This hotel features small outdoor and indoor Hawaiian-themed water activity center.

Ramada Limited
1073 Wisconsin Dells Parkway
☎   608-254-2218
dellsramada.com
Hotel features indoor pool and spa facilities and limited food service.

Luna Inn
1111 Wisconsin Dells Parkway
☎   608-253-2661
🖱 lunainn.com
Located across from Noah's Ark, this establishment features an indoor and outdoor pool, small water activity areas, a game room, and an outdoor park. (Seasonal)

Flamingo Motel & Suites
1220 Wisconsin Dells Parkway
☎   608-253-2911
🖱 dellsflamingo.com
You can't get much closer to Noah's Ark than by staying at the Flamingo Motel (it's right next door).

Skyline Hotel and Suites
1970 Wisconsin Dells Parkway
☎   608-253-4841
🖱 dellsweb.com
Hotel features indoor and outdoor pool, and is located right across the street from the Mt. Olympus amusement complex.

Days Inn Wisconsin Dells
944 U.S. Highway 12
☎   608-254-6444
🖱 dellsdaysinn.com
Establishment located just north of the main Wisconsin Dells Parkway Strip, with easy access to both Parkway and Downtown Dells. Features indoor and outdoor pool, game room, and limited food service.

Aloha Beach Resort & Suites
1370 East Hiawatha Drive
☎   608-253-4741
🖱 alohabeachresort.com
Located directly on the beach of Lake Delton. Heated indoor pool and outdoor pool. (Seasonal)

COMMERCIAL CAMPGROUNDS

The fair-weather camper will feel completely at home within these campgrounds. Many of them have wooded sites, cabins, R.V. parking capabilities, and even equipment rentals. Customize your experience to be as rustic or modern as you want.

Most campsites are seasonal; check with the establishment for any off-season or wintertime hours (when applicable).

Sherwood Forest
S352 U.S. Highway 12
☎ 608-254-7080
🖰 sherwoodforestcamping.com
This large forested campsite of oak and pine trees features many different lots, some extremely secluded-feeling. On-site there are playgrounds, video arcade, outdoor heated pool, as well as shower and laundry facilities.

Yogi Bear's Jellystone Park
S1915 Ishnala Road
☎ 608-254-2568
🖰 dellsjellystone.com
The Dells branch of this well-known commercial family campground chain features a nice-sized, exclusive outdoor waterpark, camp & R.V. sites, various log cabins for rent, many child-centric activities. It comes complete with well-known cartoon-ish ambience, restaurant, bar, and more.

Wisconsin Dells KOA
S235A Stand Rock Road
☎ 608-254-4177
🖰 wisdellskoa.com
Campground features heated pool, showers and laundry facili-

ties, store, restrooms, lots of shade, and less than one mile to Downtown Dells.

Stand Rock Campground
N570 County Road N
☎ 608-253-2169
🖰 standrock.com
A few miles north of town, on the Wisconsin River, Stand Rock Campground features over 200 camping sites (from tent to R.V.), showering and laundry facilities, a restaurant, and various family-oriented activities.

Dell Boo Family Campground
E10562 Shady Lane Road
☎ 608-356-5898
🖰 dellboo.com
About halfway between Wisconsin Dells and Baraboo is the wooded Dell Boo Family Campground (tents and R.V. hookups), which features heated swimming pool, video arcade, and washroom facilities.

Bonanza Campground
1770 Wisconsin Dells Parkway
☎ 608-254-8124
🖰 dells.com/bonanza
Perhaps the best location for a campground in the entire Wisconsin Dells, Bonanza Campground is right in the middle of the Wisconsin Dells Parkway. It is located across from the Mt. Olympus entertainment complex, and only a few blocks from Noah's Ark. Features tent and R.V. capabilities, wooded sites, heated pool, mini-golf, and shower and laundry facilities.

DOWNTOWN DELLS AREA

These hotels are located within the Downtown Dells section of town (generally a few blocks off the main strip but within walking distance of shopping and eating). These are all small motels, generally suitable for the budget-minded traveler.

Bridge View Motel
1020 River Road
☎ 608-254-6114
🖰 bridgeviewmotel.com
Small motel features views of the Upper Dells area of the Wisconsin River. (Seasonal)

Chippewa Motel
1114 East Broadway
☎ 608-253-3982
🖰 chippewamotel.com
Features outdoor pool and large indoor pool, game room, small outdoor park/playground.

Colonial Motel
606 Broadway
☎ 608-253-7771
Outdoor pool, on the Downtown Dells' main strip.

Finch Motel
811 Oak Street
☎ 608-253-4342
Just off the main Downtown Dells strip.

Fitzgerald's Motel
530 Broadway
☎ 608-253-1651
🖰 fitzgeraldsmotel.com
Small motel over 50 years old (renovated regularly); with outdoor pool.

Park Motel
715 Broadway
☎   608-254-6100
🖰 dellsparkmotel.com
Motel features an outdoor pool just off the Downtown Dells strip. (Seasonal)

Parkway Motel
223 Wisconsin Avenue
☎   608-254-7505
Motel features an old train caboose on the property, remodeled as a hot dog stand. (Seasonal)

River Road Motel
828 River Road
☎   608-254-8252
🖰 riverroadmotel.com
Just off the main Downtown Dells strip and near the River Walk.

Nearby Attractions

Central Wisconsin features a surprisingly diverse set of attractions for any traveler. Notwithstanding the way many locals milk their cheese state status, keeping sights only on the Dells themselves

> **Contents:**
> *Other Area Attractions*
> *Madison*

would deny oneself of some of the most unique attractions in America, right in the middle of its heartland. Following are some attractions good enough to warrant a somewhat lengthy trip out of the Wisconsin Dells.

OTHER AREA ATTRACTIONS

Wisconsin is very spread out; the attractions here don't fit into any particular city or zone, and some are even several hours outside of Wisconsin Dells. However, they are still within driving range and still draw crowds from the Dells area.

FRANK LLOYD WRIGHT'S HOME AND STUDIO

507 County Highway C
☎ 608-588-7900
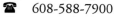 taliesinpreservation.org
The common name for this attraction is **Taliesin Preservation, Inc.** (or simply **Taliesin**), though the Taliesin building itself is only a small portion of what this massive 600-acre complex has to offer. It is located in a rural area near Spring Green, Wisconsin.

Taliesin is originally the name of a Welch bard. It means "shining brow," and it is the name Wright gave his home and studio. He began construction of his home in 1911, on the same land where his maternal family lived during the Civil War era. He moved in with his second wife at the end of that year. It started out as 32 acres, and over time the grounds expanded eventually to what is the 600 acres of today. After completing Taliesin, Wright designed another major facility for himself and his work in Scottsdale, Arizona, called Taliesin West.

It was at Taliesin where Wright designed some of his most famous buildings, notably

Fallingwater in rural Pennsylvania and the Guggenheim Museum in New York City. Wright's designs, though beautiful, are also known for being extremely fragile and thus do not hold up well to the passage of time. Therefore, Taliesin (like many of Wright's designs) is constantly being preserved and renovated.

Visitors to Taliesin are offered several levels of tours of the grounds, ranging from one hour to multiple hours. These tours consist of walking and seeing some of the sites, including the Taliesin (studio) itself, and surrounding buildings. The tours operate during the spring, summer and fall. Children under 12 are not allowed on some of the tours.

The main point of contact of the complex is the **Frank Lloyd Wright Visitor Center**. Here visitors find lots of information about Taliesin, start tours, and purchase various Wright-related books and gifts. The visitor center (like Taliesin itself) is not open during the coldest months.

(*Note:* For information on the nearby *House on the Rock*, an architectural parody of Frank Lloyd Wright and Taliesin, see that chapter elsewhere in this book.) ($$)

LITTLE A-MERRICK-A
700 East Main Street
☎ littleamerricka.com
✆ 608-655-3181

Marshall, Wisconsin, is about midway between Madison and Milwaukee, 70 miles east of Wisconsin Dells, and home to Little A-Merrick-A. This small amusement park features about 20 rides, mainly midway amusement style, and is largely designed for families with younger children.

The park features three small roller coasters, one designed especially for kids. Also among the attractions are go-karts, Tilt-a-Whirl, Wisconsin's only monorail, a miniature golf course, bumper cars & boats, and a collection of kiddie rides.

Another major highlight of the park is a three-mile train ride around the complex. A 1/3-size steam or diesel (depending on the day) train takes visitors around the amusement park, including two miles of scenic forest and wildlife and old-town settings.

Little A-Merrick-A has a main tourist season in the summer (when most of the rides are open) but there are certain holiday-time attractions that are open year-round, such as special Halloween and Christmas train rides. ($$/$$$)

MADISON

Wisconsin's capital is located about 50 miles from Wisconsin Dells. Much of the major traffic to and from Wisconsin Dells originates from Madison (for those flying into the area). With a population of over 200,000 residents, it is the second largest city in Wisconsin.

HENRY VILAS ZOO
702 South Randall Avenue
☎ 608-266-4372
🖰 vilaszoo.org
One of the top family attractions in Madison is the Henry Vilas Zoo. With a history dating back to 1904, the zoo's moderately small size (less than 50 acres) makes it a relaxing destination; it has primates, aquatic animals, giraffes, rhinos, kangaroos, camels, and other standard zoo fare. ($/$$)

OLBRICH BOTANICAL GARDENS
3330 Atwood Avenue
☎ 608-246-4550
🖰 olbrich.org
The Orbrich Botanical Gardens is a series of indoor and outdoor garden settings, which seeks to preserve many different kinds of plant life.

The **Outdoor Gardens** is about 16 acres and features an herb garden, a Rose Garden, Meadow Garden, Thai Pavilion and Garden, and more. It is open daily and features free admission.

The **Bolz Conservatory** is a glass-enclosed indoor facility which emulates a tropical environment. In addition to over 750 different kinds of plants, there is also wildlife here, including select birds, insects, and fish.

The entire Gardens is owned by the City of Madison Parks Division, and is open year-round. ($)

UNIVERSITY OF WISCONSIN-MADISON
716 Langdon Street
☎   608-263-2400
🖱 wisc.edu

Madison has been described as a major college town. The flagship university of the Wisconsin higher education system is the University of Wisconsin-Madison. It is a top national university with a massive 900-acre main campus; it enrolls over 40,000 students, which makes it one of the largest universities in the United States.

CAPITAL BUILDING
4 East Capitol Square
☎   608-266-0382

Being the state's capital, Madison has a collection of state buildings and facilities. Though "touring" these buildings is somewhat restricted and not wholly designed to be visitor-friendly (it is after all a functional government complex), it is common to at least drive by the capital, and there are surrounding grounds that are interesting for individuals or families to explore for a little while.

The House on the Rock

"Therefore whosoever heareth these sayings of mine, and doeth them, I will liken him unto a wise man, which built his house upon a rock: And the rain descended, and the floods came, and the winds blew, and beat upon that house; and it fell not: for it was founded upon a rock.

And every one that heareth these sayings of mine, and doeth them not, shall be likened unto a foolish man, which built his house upon the sand: And the rain descended, and the floods came, and the winds blew, and beat upon that house; and it fell: and great was the fall of it."

- Matthew 7:24 – 7:27

It is hard to say whether the name of Alex Jordan's unforgettable artistic installment is meant as a parody or homage to what God said, but to most visitors of Spring Green, Wisconsin, it does not matter. In the world of roadside kitsch, this is the quintessential destination. New York City art nouveau enthusiasts drool, children gawk wildly, and parents gasp in awe. In tiny Spring Green, Wisconsin, the House on the Rock is one of America's *best attractions*, roadside kitsch or otherwise. But don't take my word for it...

Contact	
☎	608-935-3639
🖱	thehouseontherock.com

WHAT IS THE HOUSE?

The House on the Rock is a 200+ acre complex near the town of Spring Green, about an hour east of Wisconsin Dells. It is part museum, part architectural feat, a hint of amusement park, but mainly, it is just plain weird. The entryway, ticket booth, and even descriptive property map give little indication as to the type of attraction that its visitors are about to see. They simply pay their money, and just go with it.

In a nutshell, the House on the Rock is an inexplicably diverse experiment in total and complete randomness. Visitors following the one-way path through the complex, mostly indoors, will come across various collections – in one room, see doll houses on display. In another room, see the world's largest carousel. In yet another room, see a collection of cars, which span the history of automobiles. There are guns, swords, organs, musical instruments, armor, and even an (indoor) antique street scene. At these collections, visitors won't see a few dozen items, or even hundreds, but literally *thousands*, covering all the walls of huge warehouse-size rooms.

HISTORY

Architectural enthusiasts will immediately recognize Spring Green, Wisconsin, as being the location of Taliesin, the home and studio of world-renown architect Frank Lloyd Wright. The inception of the House on the Rock began as kind of an architectural conquest of sorts, between the late Wright's property and his hot-headed Wisconsonian neighbor Alex Jordan, determined to out-do him.

What ultimately came about between these two nearby estates is a dichotomy of tasteful intellect and extravagant kitsch. While today Wright's Taliesin maintains its educational and historical significance, Jordan's House on the Rock draws more than *10 times* as many visitors (about *half a million* annually) with its in-your-face showiness and tack.

TALIESIN AND JORDAN

Wright began construction of Taliesin in 1911 as a place for him to live and experiment on architectural possibilities. The property began on less than 100 acres and eventually expanded to over 600 acres. Today it is a large complex of buildings of varying levels of importance to Wright's career.

However, during one particular phase of development, budding architect Alex Jordan was denied a job by Wright. Jordan took this personally, and in the 1940s he decided to show up Wright by building a house of his own. So, a few miles from Taliesin, overlooking the Wyoming Valley (south of Spring Green), Jordan came across Deer Shelter Rock, a chimney-shaped sandstone formation, and thus began a project to build a house on top of it, the style of which is generally accepted as being a spiteful parody of Wright's style.

Case in point: though the house uses much of Wright's classic compression-expansion techniques and sharp angular form, the house is grossly misshapen, the ceilings are low, the rooms are dark and very claustrophobic, and everything seems at odd angles with each other. There is a quasi-Oriental style about the décor, and yet much of the design manages to match that of Wright. But still, it sits atop a rock, and in many ways it is calling to Taliesin, "look at me, I'm better than you!" Alex Jordan's son, Alex, Jr., would eventually take over the project and succeed in turning the attraction into much more than a mere walk-through of a most unusual house.

Alex Jordan was a collector of various knick-knacks, and decided to put his collections on display for visitors wishing to tour the house. So initially when they were finished, they would step outside and get a chance to see some of these collections. But a second building wouldn't quite fit all these random items. Nor would two, or three, or ten. In fact, more than fourteen huge buildings have been constructed over the years around the original House, housing everything from dollhouses to armor.

VISITORS TO THE ROCK

Jordan never intended the house to be a tourist attraction; he built it as a kind of retreat. However, people were drawn to it. Therefore, in 1961, he opened it as an attraction and eventually began charging admission.

As the popularity grew, so did the size of the collections. Today, the original House on the Rock is but a mere fragment of this gargantuan attraction; a first step through seemingly endless rooms filled to the brim with the most random of knickknacks. In fact, the house itself is even rather dull compared to everything else; it isn't until visitors enter one of the many other compounds on the property where the fun really begins.

TOURING THE HOUSE

The House on the Rock is a self-guided tour through a largely one-way path that takes visitors around the entire complex. The house and surrounding buildings are hidden among lush wilderness; you can't see much of anything until you've paid your admission price and begun the tour. Visitors are given information upon commencing the tour as to what they will see along the journey. This section describes *some* of the various sites to behold during a visit to the House on the Rock.

THE HOUSE ON THE ROCK

The first stop on the tour is the house itself. Though it carries the namesake of the entire attraction, the house is rather small and congested, with low ceilings and a dark claustrophobic quality. It has less-than-subtle Asian influences mixed with Frank Lloyd Wright. The house is in fact so dark and claustrophobic, and the attraction in general so hidden and twisty, that visitors may forget it is perched atop a rock.

The **Infinity Room** is the most advertised – and most memorable – part of this house, even though it was added much later, in 1985. The room stretches out about 218 feet over the Wyoming Valley below. At the edge of the room, visitors can peer down and see the tops of the trees of the valley. In fact, the entire room is an illusion; visitors looking down the long corridor will think the room stretches out infinitely. It is also brightest room of the house, with over three thousand windows.

MUSICAL THINGAMAJIGS

There is little interaction between visitors and the exhibits, with one very notable exception: the automated music machines. Along the path are dozens of these robotic musical exhibits. Visitors pop in some money, and these wacky contraptions come to life, and play songs – these not like a radio or speakers, but rather are *actual acoustic instruments* that are wired up to play one specific song. Some of them are small, with only a few instruments, whereas others take up entire rooms.

For example, in one classically decorated room, an entire orchestra – woodwinds, brass, and strings, are wired up to play one song whenever a visitor deposits money. The instruments tend to be out of tune, which gives these otherwise popular songs (such as Bolero and Hungarian Rhapsody) a very eerie mechanical feel. There are over thirty such displays scattered throughout the house and neighboring buildings. These are totally pointless, yet somehow manage to fit perfectly with the artistry of the entire attraction.

MILL HOUSE

As visitors follow the path, they come across the Mill House. Inside, they see a collection of dolls, odd piggy banks, guns, and pieces of armor.

STREET OF YESTERDAY

This is not Disneyland's Main Street, U.S.A.; however visitors will be oddly familiar with this unusual section of the tour. It is a re-creation of a late-19th century American main street (Disney's theme park re-creation is of the turn of the 20th century). Unlike Disneyland, however, it is indoor, a perpetual twilight, and the attention is to detail, not to con-

sumerism. Gas lamps line the brick street, which is lined with genuine antiquities of the period, including a police station, various shops and even a tiny movie theater playing silent films. Visitors cannot enter most of these "shops," but they can see much through the windows.

NAUTICAL ARTIFACTS

Called **Heritage of the Sea**, this huge building houses a massive artificial whale-like creature seemingly integrated into the building's structure. The whale is about 200-feet long and occupies several stories of the building. Also in this building are various nautical recreations (such as boats), and a few additional "smaller" exhibits that have nothing to do to with the sea.

WORLD'S LARGEST CAROUSEL

It is perhaps unusual that the world's largest operational carousel is located in Spring Green (not, say, Orlando), and is not ride-able. It is perhaps more unusual that this carousel does not have on itself a single horse – but it does have 269 other animals and creatures, and 20,000 lights. The horses are attached to the wall of the room – collected from other carousels. This room also contains other pieces of carousel memorabilia.

TRANSPORTATION

The House on the Rock features many displays of transportation, including automobiles, aviation, and nautical craft. In one room, cars and other modes of transportation are on display.

ORGAN ROOM

Perhaps the creepiest and coolest room in the whole complex, the Organ Room is a walk through what can only be described as a dungeon of pipes. Visitors walk on platforms, walkways, and bridges as they intimately explore some of the largest pipe organs ever created. It resembles a dimly lit factory; and the eerie sounds of organ noises echo incessantly. The room is positively huge, and the path allows visitors to explore several sections of these massive instruments up close and personal.

CONVENIENCE STOPS

Along the tour, visitors will encounter three food stops, with various delectable fast-food options like pizza, hot dogs, candy, ice cream, and other delights. Of course, there are also gift shops along the **Display Garden** promenade where all of your essential (is that a word that can be used to describe *any*thing here?) gift products may be purchased.

RESORT COMPLEX

The House on the Rock has two additional nearby locations, each about seven miles away: the Inn and the Resort.

About seven miles away from the House on the Rock attraction is the newer House on the Rock Resort, which includes an inn and golf complex. Here, visitors wishing to stay close to the attraction will be delighted to find lots of modern resort amenities. The design of these establishments is of course reminiscent of the House attraction, with more of an emphasis on Frank Lloyd Wright's influence, and not the parody. Of course, the resort offers packages that include admission to the House on the Rock exhibit.

THE HOUSE ON THE ROCK INN
3591 Highway 23
☎   608-935-3711
In Dodgeville, the House on the Rock Inn provides a place for people seeing the attraction to relax. The hotel features two sections: a main lodge and a north lodge, which combined offer well over 100 rooms. The whole complex has several indoor pool areas (one of them is actually a water playground), a video arcade and fitness center, and other hotel-centric amenities. The Main Lodge is bigger than the North Lodge but they both can stand independently.

THE HOUSE ON THE ROCK RESORT & GOLF COURSE
400 Springs Drive
☎   608-935-3639
About seven miles away from the attraction itself, the House on the Rock Resort & Golf Course is for visitors who want to experience the House on the Rock, and still have time for golf. Though part of the House on the Rock, this facility stands alone as being a golfing destination (as the name suggests).

The main resort is close to the Wisconsin River, and is designed with the outdoor sports enthusiast in mind. It is an upscale establishment following the design style of Frank Lloyd Wright. There are 80 suites on the premises, as well as a fitness center, several indoor pools, tennis courts, whirlpool and Jacuzzi, and many miles of naturalistic hiking trails. The resort also allows for easy access to Wright's Taliesin.

In addition to the main resort complex, there are 27 holes of golf. Eighteen of them encompass one professional course, the **Springs Course**. The other 9 holes, called the **North Nine**, are just as challenging but allow for a shorter game. The course also has a restaurant, bar, and pro shop on the premises.

CONCLUSION

I have found it both unfortunate and incredible that such a unique and wonderful attraction is located so far away from places where this type of art would be most appreciated.

Though it has nothing to do with the Wisconsin Dells, since you as a visitor have made it this far, I highly suggest that you take a day away from the Dells and see this one-of-a-kind masterpiece.

Need an idea as to how a Wisconsin Dells vacation would be? This section provides some examples of the various kinds of vacations that visitors may enjoy at Wisconsin Dells.

SUMMER WATER FUN

When to Go: July or August
Time: 2 or 3 Nights

In the dog days of summer, waterparks are the #1 attraction at Wisconsin Dells. Thousands upon thousands of people visit these facilities every day, largely of the family and young-adult-friends sect.

Unlike many theme parks, water parks do not necessarily need multiple days of enjoyment. Though they can be huge, the fun does not necessarily involve waiting in a waterslide line, but rather splashing around and idling about. One full day at a waterpark is perfect for a family or friends.

Arrive in the afternoon; don't worry about cramming in fun after arrival. There are lots of things to do in the Dells that don't take an entire day, or even an hour. Arrive at your hotel or motel. Since it's the summertime, you may not need to invest in a huge resort with an indoor waterpark; just at a local motel near your favorite attraction. Spend the evening puttering around, perhaps taking in a good haunted house or mini-golf session.

Plan to spend the next full day at a major outdoor waterpark; this could be either Noah's Ark or the Family Land part of Mt. Olympus. Those wishing for dry attractions as well (such as roller coasters) may consider Family Land/Mt. Olympus, though Noah's Ark has considerably more water attractions.

Waterparks close well before dusk, so plan on an evening activity as well. Tommy Bartlett's Thrill Show has evening performances, and the show is a family crowd-pleaser. The restaurants along the Wisconsin Dells Parkway offer all kinds of pre-show family dining. After dark, a trek to Downtown Dells offers up some bars, smaller restaurants and after-hours attractions.

A second full day may be booked to plan for inclement

weather, or for visitors wishing to explore other parts of the Dells (such as tours of the Wisconsin River or a more full-featured Downtown area experience).

WINTER WATER FUN
Time: 1 or 2 Nights
When to Go: December through February

A surprising number of indoor waterpark attractions have been cropping up all over the nation; and Wisconsin Dells seems to be at the heart of this new trend. With major indoor waterpark resorts such as Kalahari and Great Wolf Lodge, season is no longer a factor for enjoying waterparks in wintery weather.

Arriving at Wisconsin Dells in the dead of winter is a stark change from the summertime; roads and buildings are blanketed with as much as several feet of snow, many of the smaller resorts are closed, and most of the attractions have shut down. However, the indoor waterpark resorts are open, brightly lit, and in full swing! As such, winter water enjoyment within the Dells *almost* requires that you stay at one of these major resorts. Although some allow for visitors to pay for a one-day admission to their resi-dent indoor parks, others only allow hotel guests to access them. Additionally, these resorts have many other on-site amenities and activities, so braving the outdoors is not integral for fun.

Arrive at the hotel at any time in the afternoon, since the indoor parks tend to be open later than would be expected (sometimes 9 or 10PM) and spend time exploring the resort! As much of the rest of the Dells is shut down, this makes a stay more relaxing. There are a few wintertime fun stops open throughout Wisconsin Dells other than the resorts; these are mainly restaurants and the smaller, indoor attractions. Not as much time is needed as there is less to do, so a short one or two night vacation might be all that is needed.

THE GREAT OUTDOORS
Time: 1 or 2 Nights
When to Go: Anytime; different seasons offer different experiences.

As the unofficial "gateway" to the famous Northwoods of Wisconsin, the Dells naturally (no pun intended) offers a lot of nature-loving outdoor activities during all seasons. In the summer there is camping, hiking, boating activities and swimming. In the wintertime, there is sledding, cross-country skiing, and snowmobiling. During any season, horseback riding, fishing, and even camping may be available.

Visitors using the Dells for its outdoor activities tend to be from nearby; it is an accessible place for city dwellers yet not so out in the boonies that a short drive won't bring travelers back. It's kind of a fair-weather nature place.

WITHOUT THE KIDS
Time: 1 or 2 Nights
When to Go: Spring or Fall
If you plan on heading over to the Dells without children, there are factors to consider: visiting in the middle of summer will bring about crowded clans of families; visiting in the winter offers little to do except for the indoor waterparks (which are frequented almost exclusively by families).

Author Recommendations

For information about the author, please see the end of this book.

This is my favorite section of the book! Here, I get to tell you my favorite attractions, things to do, places to go, itineraries, and whatever else catches my fancy. The information here is *personal*. What do I like to do? What are my favorite attractions, hotels, restaurants, etc.?

I have been visiting Wisconsin Dells for as long as I can remember. My first memories, or course, are in a waterpark, but I have since grown to love all aspects of this quintessential Midwest tourist destination. I am happy that there is a town like Wisconsin Dells. While most of the focus is on families, there is a lot to do here for anybody with sense of good old-fashioned commercial fun.

WHEN TO GO

Although "summertime" might be the first instinctual reaction as to when the best time would be to visit Wisconsin Dells, consider this: summer is only the best to,e to visit when you or your family/friends intend to visit the outdoor waterparks. Plus, it will be very crowded and hotel prices will be at their max. With that in mind, I very much enjoy a visit to the dells in the spring or the fall. Waterparks may (or may not) be open, the weather is cooler, and yet the other non-aquatic attractions are still open and in full-swing, like the amusement park and boat attractions. In fact, a visit during April or October is best for me, since many of the attractions are still open, and should I want a watery activity, the indoor waterparks will always be open.

HOW TO GET THERE

Having a car (or access to some mode of personal vehicular transportation) within the Dells area is almost a requirement, unless you plan your trip well enough to locate yourself within a resort or section of the city where you don't need to travel around much. Taking a train into the Dells may seem like a more frugal and easy option (since there is a station right in the middle of Downtown Dells), but the station has minimal amenities and you will need a car anyway, so only take a train (or bus, for that matter) if you have arrangements for other transportation upon arrival.

Chicago has a big and busy airport complex, but the Milwaukee airport is markedly closer to the Dells than Chicago. Madison has an airport as well, but flights to Madison are more regional and may require a more expensive fare with fewer travel options.

FAVORITE ATTRACTIONS

One of my favorite aspects of Wisconsin Dells is the ability to simply tinker around arbitrarily. Most of the attractions don't require any significant time commitment; they can be enjoyed within the course of a few hours or less. That way, visitors can enjoy the ambience, walk around, see what there is to see, etc.

However, before that, it is still important to see the natural Dells themselves. Therefore, any major boat ride (duck or otherwise) along the Wisconsin River or Lake Delton is top priority on my travel agenda. Afterwards, I also try to catch the Tommy Bartlett Thrill Show if I'm in the

mood for a sit-down experience. However, after those almost obligatory attractions, I am free to roam about.

I have always been a fan of Ripley's museums so one of my first stops in the Dells is the Downtown area. The shops are fun too, but all the merchandise gets a bit repetitive after a while.

If I happen to be in the Dells with a group of people in the summertime, we will almost certainly hit either Family Land or Noah's Ark. Also, the Mt. Olympus go-karts and roller coasters are great places to spend some time. In the evening or later that night, Pirate's Cove Adventure Golf is fun for just about anyone.

SPENDING THE NIGHT

In my opinion, the indoor waterpark resorts of Wisconsin Dells are the best thing to happen to family vacations since Disney World. They are still in their infancy and will probably undergo significant re-development through their maturation process, but what a start! I imagine they will, one day, pair up with (or rival) casino resorts.

But you don't have to enjoy the waterpark to enjoy one of these places. Some of the resorts are more family-oriented than other. For example, Great Wolf Lodge has an almost cartoonish and endearing quality suitable for young children. On the other hand, the Wilderness Resort has a full-scale golf course as well as indoor waterpark, which can cater to adults as well as children. Whatever your desire, these are unique resort complexes that are worth a look during any season (with their increasing popularity nationwide, however, they may not be unique for long).

However, staying at a large resort may be a detriment, because it draws away from a more traditional Dells vacation — that is, staying at a smaller motel. Both choices of lodging have their advantages and disadvantages.

There are many sources for additional information regarding Wisconsin Dells. This book is merely a piece of the literary patchwork that allows those desiring to learn as much as they want. Following is a list of additional sources that will fill the gaps of this publication, as well as provide

Contents:
Books
Websites
List of Attractions
Historic Photographs
Glossary

more accurate and thorough information. Many of these sources were used to gather information contained in this book.

BOOKS

There is lots of information about Wisconsin Dells as sections of larger travel guides, such as those about Wisconsin in general. Though these books are generally not as thorough as this one, they provide a second perspective on some of the more popular attractions within the Dells area.

Given the Dells' unique position as a tourist town, it is best to look in books dedicated to "odd" or "unusual" Wisconsin sites, as the more general travel books tend to breeze over the Dells to talk about more conventional destinations like Green Bay, Madison, and Milwaukee.

Note: Listed ISBNs are for a more recent version of the book as determined at press time; later versions may be available.

The Great Wisconsin Tour Book
Published by Trail Books
October, 2000
ISBN 0-9150248-4-5
With a focus on Wisconsin road trips, this book contains a chapter on the Wisconsin Dells/Baraboo area.

Oddball Wisconsin
Pub. by Chicago Review Press
April, 2001
ISBN 1-5565237-6-9
This book has a great section highlighting some of the best attraction in the Wisconsin Dells, including waterparks, resorts, and the ducks.

Wisconsin Curiosities
Published by Globe Pequot
September, 2004
ISBN 0-7627304-0-4
This book covers a wide range of Wisconsin attractions, with some detail on Wisconsin Dells and the Baraboo region. Some articles go rather in-depth.

Moon Handbooks Wisconsin
Published by Moon Handbooks
January, 2005
ISBN 1-5669160-0-3
Though more of a general Wisconsin book, it does have an entire chapter on Central Wisconsin (sans Madison, which has its own chapter) that discusses the Dells, Baraboo, and surrounding area.

WEBSITES

There are some great Internet resources on Wisconsin Dells. When planning your trip, these websites provide additional information – in some cases, it may even be possible to purchase tickets online. These websites are, of course, in addition to the ones that are listed with the individual attractions in this book.

WISCONSIN DELLS VISITOR & CONVENTION BUREAU
☎ 800-254-4293
🖰 wisdells.com
This extremely comprehensive website contains massive amounts of information about the attractions, parks, accommodations, and much more within the Dells area.

DELLS DOT COM
🖰 dells.com
Part of a larger web entity dedicated to travel in Wisconsin, Dells Dot Com has information about lots of Dells and area attractions, including some coupons and discounts for the more popular ones.

DELLS PACKAGES
🖰 dellspackages.com
Web site features a wide variety of vacation packages for different tastes, including seasonal packages and off-season (wintertime) deals.

WISCONSIN-DELLS.NET

⌐ wisconsin-dells.net

This site is mostly a directory of attractions and accommodations, with helpful phone numbers and web site links.

WISCONSIN HISTORICAL SOCIETY

⌐ wisconsinhistory.org

This site contains lots of great information on the history of Wisconsin. In particular, it has many, many photographs of the Wisconsin Dells taken by H. H. Bennett.

LIST OF ATTRACTIONS ─────────────

Following is a list of all the attractions in the Wisconsin Dells area that are detailed in this book, and their corresponding page number.

The Northeast	18	Packing Light vs. Packing	
The Southeast	18	Right	25
The Midwest	18	Changes of Clothes	26
The Southwest	19	Toiletries	26
The West Coast	20	Medications	26
Summertime	20	Trip Specifics	26
Off-Season and Winter	20	Flying	27
Holiday Season	21	Driving	28
Wintertime	21	Basic Hotel Amenities	29
Chamber of Commerce	21	Bed & Breakfasts	30
Visitor's Bureau	22	Motels	30
Independently printed Travel		Hostels	30
Guides	22	Resorts	31
Travel Agents	22	Fast Food	31
The Internet	23	Buffets	32
Travel Fares	23	Casual Dining	32
Accommodation Prices	24	Fine Dining	32
Food Money	24	Tipping	32
Attraction Money	24	Formation of the Dells	34
Spending Money	25		

Early Inhabitants – Effigy
Mound Builders 35
Native Americans and
European Settlements 36
Kilbourn City 36
Ducks 37
Devil's Lake 38
H. H. Bennett 40
Tommy Bartlett 41
Families with Children 42
Couples 42
Singles and Friends 43
Wisconsin Dells Parkway 44
Downtown Dells / Dells River
District 44
Lake Delton 44
Baraboo 45
See the Dells' Rock Formations
45
Go to a Waterpark (or
Amusement Park) 46
Go Shopping 46
Miscellaneous 47
Stand Rock 47
Witches Gulch 47
Rocky Islands 48
By Car 48
By Air 49
By Train or Bus 49
Resorts 50
Motels 50
Campgrounds 51
Summer 51
Fall 51
Winter 52
Spring 52

"Leaping the Chasm" and
Stand Rock 57
Drawing Tourists 58
Landscape Photographs 58
Original Wisconsin Ducks 65
Dells Army Ducks 66
Dells Boat Tours 66
Aqua Adventures Jet Airboats
68
Original Dells Experience Jet
Boats 68
Lost Canyon Tours 69
Monster Truck World 69
Waterpark Primer 70
Noah's Ark Waterpark 72
Mt. Olympus Water & Theme
Park 73
Riverview Park & Waterworld
74
Timber Falls Adventure Park 75
Storybook Gardens &
Timbavati Wildlife Park 75
Extreme World 76
Great Wolf Lodge 78
Kalahari Resorts 79
Wilderness Hotel & Golf
Resort 80
Polynesian Resort Hotel 81
Treasure Island 82
Copa Cabana 82
Atlantis Waterpark Hotel 83
RainTree Resort 83
Camelot Hotel & Suites 83
Grand Marquis Resort Hotel
& Suites 84
Meadowbrook Resort 84

Canyon Creek Riding Stable 85
OK Corral Riding Stable   86
Red Ridge Ranch   86
International Crane
Foundation   87
Wisconsin Deer Park   88
Alligator Alley   88
B & H Trout Farm   88
River's Edge Resort   89
Vertical Illusions   89
Dells Water Sports / Mirror
Lake Rentals   89
Beaver Springs Fishing Park 90
Boo Canoe & Raft   90
Mirror Lake State Park   91
Devil's Lake State Park   91
Ripley's Believe It or Not!
Museum   93
H. H. Bennett Studio and
History Center   94
Circus World Museum   94
Museum of Historic Torture
Devices   95
Tommy Bartlett's Exploratory
       96
Top Secret   96
The Wonder Spot   97
Wizard Quest   97
Alien Planet   97
Dungeon of Horrors   98
Ghost Out-Post   98
Loony Bin   98
Haunted Mansion   98
Dells Mining Co.   99
Laser Storm of Wisconsin Dells
       99

Mid-Continent Railway
Museum   100
Black Bart's Old #9   100
Riverside & Great Northern
Railroad   101
Tommy Bartlett Thrill Show
       101
Wisconsin Opry   102
Rick Wilcox Theater   102
Crystal Grand Music Theatre
       103
Fab '50s Live   103
Thunder Valley Inn Dinner
Show   103
Al Ringling Theatre   104
Ho-Chunk Casino   105
Wollersheim Winery   106
saloons of the Downtown Dells
       106
Christmas Mountain Village
Golf   107
Coldwater Canyon Golf
Course   107
Pinecrest Golf Course   107
Wilderness Woods Golf Club
       108
Trappers Turn Golf Club   108
Spring Brook Golf Resort   108
Swiss Maid Fudge   109
Original Wisconsin Dells
Fudge   109
Kernel Popcorn's Factory   109
Candy Corner   109
Grandma's Original Fudge 109
Goody Goody Gum Drop   109

Pirate's Cove Adventure Golf 110
Big Sky Twin Drive-In Theatre 110
Paint It! Pottery Shop 111
Old River & Totem Pole
Mini-Golf 111
Woman-Dozing a Democrat 112
Frank Lloyd Wright's Home
and Studio 125
Little A-Merrick-A 126
Henry Vilas Zoo 127
Olbrich Botanical Gardens 127
University of Wisconsin-
Madison 128
Capital Building 128
Taliesin and Jordan 130
Visitors to the Rock 131
The House on the Rock 132
Musical Thingamajigs 132
Mill House 133
Street of Yesterday 133
Nautical Artifacts 133
World's Largest Carousel 133
Transportation 134
Organ Room 134
Convenience Stops 134
The House on the Rock Inn 135
The House on the Rock Resort
& Golf Course 135
Summer Water Fun 137
Winter Water Fun 138
The Great Outdoors 138
Without the Kids 139
When to Go 140
How to Get There 140
Favorite Attractions 141
Spending the Night 141
Wisconsin Dells Visitor &
Convention Bureau 144
Dells Dot Com 144
Dells Packages 144
Wisconsin-Dells.net 145
Wisconsin Historical Society 145

LIST OF HISTORIC PHOTOGRAPHS

Following are the sources and/or credits for the various historic and legacy photographs used throughout this book. Unless otherwise stated, all photos used are in the public domain.

"Boating in the Wisconsin Dells"
Copyright c1901 by C. H. Graves; The Universal Photo Art Company. Library of Congress Prints & Photographs Division

"Inkstand, Lower Dells"
Copyright c1900 by H. H. Bennett

"Inkstand and Sugar Bowl, Lower Dells"
Copyright c1885 by H. H. Bennett

"Jaws of the Wisconsin Dells"
Copyright 1894 by H. H. Bennett. Library of Congress Prints & Photographs Division

"Leaping the Chasm"
Copyright c1886 by H. H. Bennett. Wisconsin Historical Society, No. 2101. Used with Permission

"Looking out of Boat Cave" (Page xx)
Copyright c1875-1895 by H. H. Bennett

"The Narrows, Dells of the Wisconsin"
Copyright 1900 by H. H. Bennett. Library of Congress Prints & Photographs Division

"Stand Rock – showing top"
Copyright c1875-1895 by H. H. Bennett

"Yell, or Go Down!"
From George W. Peck's Woman-Dozing a Democrat.

Index

A

Accommodations, 119
Air, 49
Al Ringling Theatre, 104
Alakai Hotel, 120
Alex Jordan, 129, 130, 131
Alien Planet, 97
Alligator Alley, 88
Aloha Beach Resort, 121
Amtrak, 49
Amusement Park, 46, 72
Animal Encounters, 87
Animals and Nature, 85
Aqua Adventures Jet Airboats, 68
Area Attractions, 93, 125
Atlantis Waterpark Hotel, 83

B

B & H Trout Farm, 88
Baraboo, 15, 44, 45, 87, 90, 92,
    94, 100, 102, 104, 105, 122,
    143, 144
Bars, 118
Beaver Springs Fishing Park, 90
Bennett, 40, 56, 57, 58, 67, 94
Big Sky Twin Drive-In, 110, 111
Boat Tours, 47, 58, 64, 67
Boating, 54, 88, 148
Boating and Fishing, 88
Bonanza Campground, 123
Boo Canoe & Raft, 90
Books, 143
Bridge View Motel, 123
Bus, 49

C

Camelot Hotel & Suites, 83
Campgrounds, 51, 121
Candy Corner, 109
Canyon Creek Riding Stable, 85
Capital Building, 128
Car, 48
Casino, 105
Charles River, 64
Chippewa Motel, 123
Christmas Mountain Village Golf,
    107
Circus World Museum, 45, 91,
    94, 95
Coldwater Canyon Golf Course,
    107
Colonial Motel, 123
Copa Cabana, 82
Couples, 42, 52
Crystal Grand Music Theatre, 103

D

Dane County Regional Airport, 49
Days Inn, 121
Del-Bar, 117
Dell Boo Family Campground,
    122
Dells Army Ducks, 66
Dells Boat Tours, 66, 67, 68
Dells Early Photography, 54
Dells Mining Co., 99
Dells River District, 44
Dells Tours, 64
Dells Water Sports, 89

Display Garden, 134
Downtown Dells, 42, 43, 44, 46, 49, 52, 57, 74, 93, 106, 111, 116, 118, 119, 121, 122, 123, 124, 137, 141
Drawing Tourists, 58
Ducks, 37, 38, 65, 66, 67
Dungeon of Horrors, 98

E

Early Inhabitants, 35
Eating, 117
Econo Lodge Wisconsin Dells, 120
Essen Haus German Restaurant, 118
Extreme World, 76

F

Fall, 51, 139
Families with Children, 42
Famous Residents, 40
Fishing, 90
Flamingo Motel, 121
Formation of the Dells, 34
Frank Lloyd Wright, 91, 117, 125, 126, 130, 132, 134, 135
Fudge, 108, 109
Fun Things, 110

G

General Mitchell International Airport, 49
George Wilbur Peck, 111
Getting Around, 49
Getting There, 48
Ghost Out-Post, 98
Go to a Waterpark, 46

golf, 46, 52, 72, 80, 94, 107, 108, 110, 111, 126, 134, 135, 142
Goody Goody Gum Drop, 109
Grand Marquis Resort, 84
Great Outdoors, 138
Great Wolf Lodge, 46, 78, 79, 81, 138, 142
Greyhound, 49
Grown-Ups, 104

H

H. H. Bennett, 40, 41, 47, 54, 55, 56, 94, 115, 145, 149
H. H. Bennett Studio, 94
Haunted Mansion, 98
Henny Penny, 118
Henry Vilas Zoo, 127
Hilton Garden Inn, 120
History of the Dells, 34
Ho-Chunk Casino, 43, 45, 105
Horseback Riding, 85
House on the Rock, 52, 116, 126, 129, 130, 131, 132, 134, 135
House on the Rock Inn, 135
House on the Rock Resort & Golf Course, 135

I

Indoor Waterpark Resorts, 78
Infinity Room, 132
Introduction, 11
Ishnala Restaurant, 117

K

Kalahari Resorts, 79
Kilbourn City, 36, 37, 40, 56, 112
Klondike Kavern, 80
KOA, 122

L

Lake Delton, 15, 41, 43, 44, 45,
    48, 64, 66, 85, 88, 89, 91, 102,
    117, 120, 121, 141
Lakeside Motel, 120
Landscape Photographs, 58
Laser Storm of Wisconsin Dells,
    99
Leaping the Chasm, 40, 56, 57,
    149
Little A-Merrick-A, 126
Little Links, 108
Live Shows, 101
Loony Bin, 98
Lower Dells, 64, 65, 66, 67, 149
Luna Inn, 121

M

Madison, 33, 43, 48, 49, 126, 127,
    128, 141, 143, 144
Master Blaster, 79
Mayflower Motel, 120
Meadowbrook Resort, 84
Mid-Continent Railway Museum,
    100
Mill House, 133
MIR Space Station, 96
Mirror Lake, 89, 91, 117
Mirror Lake Rentals, 89
Monster Truck World, 69
Motels, 50
Mr. Pancake, 118
Mt. Olympus, 73, 74, 83, 121,
    123, 137, 141
Museum of Historic Torture
    Devices, 95
Museums, 93, 100

N

Native Americans, 36
Natural Features, 47
Nautical Artifacts, 133
Northwoods, 80, 85, 118, 138

O

Oaks Golf Course, 107
OK Corral Riding Stable, 86
Olbrich Botanical Gardens, 127
Old River & Totem Pole Mini-
    Golf, 111
Organ Room, 134
Orientation, 43
Original Dells Experience Jet
    Boats, 68
Original Wisconsin Dells Fudge,
    109
Original Wisconsin Ducks, 65
Other Dells Experiences, 69

P

Paint It! Pottery Shop, 111
Panoramic Photography, 55
Park Motel, 124
Parkway Motel, 124
Peck, 111, 149
Photographs, 94, 148, 149
Photography, 54
Pinecrest Golf Course, 107
Pines Golf Course, 107
Polynesian Resort Hotel, 81
Public transportation, 49

R

Ramada Limited, 121
Red Ridge Ranch, 86

Research, 14
Resorts, 50, 70
Restaurants, 117, 118
Rick Wilcox Theater, 102, 103
River Road Motel, 124
Riverside & Great Northern
    Railroad, 101
Riverview Park, 74, 109
Rocky Islands, 48

S

Seasons, 51
Sherwood Forest, 122
Shopping, 46
Showboat Saloon, 106
Singles and Friends, 43
Skinner, 38
Skyline Hotel, 121
Sleeping, 117
Spending the Night, 50, 141
splashdowns, 64
Spring, 52, 108, 125, 129, 130,
    131, 133, 139
Stand Rock, 40, 47, 57, 58, 67,
    75, 89, 94, 115, 122, 149
Stand Rock Campground, 122
State Parks, 91
Stereoscopic Photography, 54
Storybook Gardens, 75, 76
Street of Yesterday, 133
Summer, 51, 137
Summer Water Fun, 137
Sweets, 108
Swiss Maid Fudge, 109

T

Taliesin, 125, 126, 130, 131, 135

Thunder Valley Inn Dinner Show,
    103
Timbavati Wildlife Park, 75, 76
Timber Falls Adventure Park, 75
Tommy Bartlett, 40, 41, 42, 44,
    45, 82, 96, 101, 137, 141
Tommy Bartlett Thrill Show, 42,
    45, 101, 141
Top Secret, 96
Train, 49, 100
Train Experiences, 100
Trappers Turn Golf Club, 108

U

University of Wisconsin, 128
Upper Dells, 64, 65, 66, 67, 68,
    89, 123

V

Vertical Illusions, 89

W

Walk-Through Attractions, 95
Waterpark, 52, 70, 72, 73, 77, 83
Waterpark Primer, 70
Waterpark Resorts, 77
Waterworld, 74
Websites, 14, 144
Whispering Pines Restaurant, 108
Who Visits Wisconsin Dells, 42
Wild West, 80
Wilderness Hotel, 80
Wilderness Woods Golf Club, 81,
    108
Winter, 52, 92, 138
Winter Water Fun, 138
Wisconsin Deer Park, 88

Wisconsin Dells Parkway, 15, 42,
43, 44, 45, 65, 66, 69, 72, 73,
74, 75, 76, 82, 83, 84, 88, 93,
96, 98, 99, 101, 102, 117, 118,
119, 120, 121, 123, 137
Wisconsin Opry, 102
Wisconsin River, 33, 34, 35, 37,
38, 43, 44, 45, 46, 47, 48, 57,
58, 64, 65, 66, 68, 74, 88, 89,
106, 122, 123, 135, 138, 141
Witches Gulch, 47, 48, 67, 68
Without the Kids, 139
Wizard Quest, 97
Wollersheim Winery, 106
Woman-Dozing a Democrat, 112,
149
Wonder Spot, 97

About the Author

Dirk Vander Wilt is a true fan of the American Tourist Trap. From the tackiness of the amusement piers on the Jersey Shore, to the endless rows of gift shops in Orlando and Myrtle Beach, to the water parks of the Wisconsin Dells, to the wax museums of Niagara Falls, Dirk finds fun in places devoted to fun! Born in Chicago, he holds academic degrees in film production and music composition, and has a particular liking for Disney parade music and ambient scores (or what he calls "rock music" – music coming from hidden speakers). He lives in New York City.

NOTES:

NOTES:

NOTES:

NOTES:

NOTES:

NOTES:

NOTES:

NOTES:

Titles are available or coming soon. See website for details.

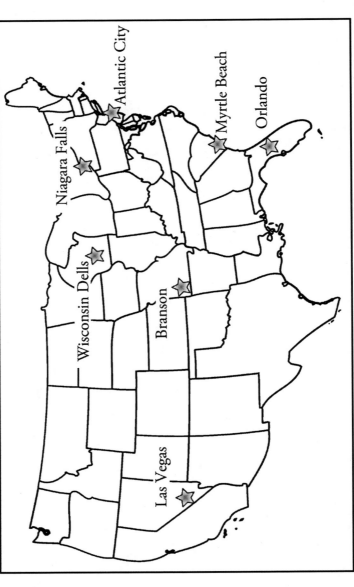

Niagara Falls

Atlantic City

Myrtle Beach

Orlando

Wisconsin Dells

Branson

Las Vegas

Parkscape Press is an imprint of Channel Lake, Inc.